Wearing Purple

Wearing Purple

Lydia Lewis Alexander

Marilyn Hill Harper

Otis Holloway Owens

Mildred Lucas Patterson

HARMONY BOOKS/NEW YORK

WE PROUDLY DEDICATE THIS BOOK
TO OUR SONS WHO HAVE INDIVIDUALLY
ENHANCED OUR LIVES:

Bryant, Harry, Hill, James, Judson, and Roger

Front cover and title page photographs: Pictured from left to right
are Mildred Lucas Patterson, Marilyn Hill Harper,
Otis Holloway Owens, and Lydia Lewis Alexander.

Grateful acknowledgment is made to print letters from Lydia's
mother, Flora Laird Lewis, and sister, Gwendolyn Lewis Harllee.
All rights reserved. Used by permission.

Published by Harmony Books, a division of Crown Publishers, Inc.,
201 East 50th Street, New York, New York 10022.
Member of the Crown Publishing Group.

Random House, Inc. New York, Toronto, London,
Sydney, Auckland

http://www.randomhouse.com/

Printed in the United States of America

Design by Lynne Amft

Library of Congress Cataloging-in-Publication Data
is available upon request.

ISBN 0-517-70834-5

10 9 8 7 6 5 4 3 2 1

First Edition

Contents

Acknowledgments 7
Introduction 9
"Wearing Purple" 10

PART I: *Old, Fat, and Forgetful* 11

Searching 12 *Almost Sixty* 13 *Old, Fat, and Forgetful* 14
Buried Navel 15 *Middle-Age Spread* 16 *The "M" Word* 17
Okay over Fifty 18 *Sexuality* 19 *No Love Lost* 20 *Get a Grip* 21 *After PMS* 23 *Lost Option* 25 *Nobody Knows* 26
First I Cry 28 *Not in My Backyard* 29 *Frustration* 31 *Late-Life Parental Frustration* 32 *Sounding Boards* 34 *Venting Frustration* 35 *Mama's Caregiver* 36 *Ups and Downs* 37
Support from Afar? 39 *Care for the Caregiver* 40 *Pondering Loneliness* 42 *Care and Share* 44 *Learning to Cope* 45
Finding Time 46 *Decisions, Decisions* 47

PART II: *Letting Go* 49

Letting Go 50 *Missed Opportunities* 51 *Devastating Losses* 52
Veen's Dream 53 *Facing Life Alone* 54 *Mamma Transformed* 55 *Who Am I?* 56 *Peace* 57 *Thanks* 58 *Final Journey* 59 *Struggling for Strength* 60 *The Biggest Loss* 61
A Heavy Heart 62 *Passing the Torch* 63 *Losing Stanli* 64
Losing Jo 65 *Diving Headfirst* 69 *Leaving Iowa* 70
Honorable Closure 71 *New Beginnings* 73 *Waiting for Clarity* 75 *Restoring Hope* 76

PART III: *The Three-Legged Stool* 77

Relationships 78 *Empty Nest* 79 *Family Fantasy* 80 *"Don't Be No Fool"* 81 *Manipulative Mentor* 83 *Inspirational Mentor* 84 *Mama Luke* 85 *Muddied Relationship* 86 *The Jerk* 87 *Men Friends* 89 *Solitude/Togetherness* 91 *Walking*

Sticks 93 🖋 *Not Too Close* 95 🖋 *Staying Afloat* 96 🖋 *Alone Forever?* 97 🖋 *Indecision* 98 🖋 *A Three-Legged Stool* 99 *Lover or Friend?* 101 🖋 *Wedding Vows* 102

P A R T I V : *Ending Midlife Mental Mess* 103

Hints of Purple 104 🖋 *Cause to Celebrate* 105 🖋 *Appreciate Self* 107 🖋 *Proud Friend* 108 🖋 *A Stabilizing Force* 109 🖋 *A Fine 29* 110 🖋 *Celebrate Life* 112 🖋 *Reunions* 113 🖋 *Strengths Acknowledged* 114 🖋 *Lydia's Sister's Letter* 115 🖋 *Acknowledgment* 117 🖋 *Special Gifts* 118 🖋 *The Real Caregiver* 119 *Green Tigers* 121 🖋 *Joy Is...* 122 🖋 *Joyful Years* 124 🖋 *Wedding Flashback* 126 🖋 *Joy Anyhow* 127

P A R T V : *Fit at Fifty* 129

Fit at Fifty Plus 130 🖋 *Working Out* 131 🖋 *Changing Bodies* 132 *Slow Leak* 134 🖋 *The Klutz* 136 🖋 *Writing Therapy* 137 *Restoration* 138 🖋 *Whatever Fits* 139 🖋 *Battling the Bulge* 140 *Supreme Sacrifices* 141 🖋 *Running Again* 142 🖋 *Heart Scares* 143 *Retail Therapy* 144 🖋 *Dress for Comfort* 145 🖋 *Personal Style* 146 *Spiritual Fitness* 147 🖋 *Renewal* 149

P A R T V I : *Birth of a Circle* 151

Birth of a Circle 152 🖋 *Lost in Chaos* 153 🖋 *Focus* 154 🖋 *Clear Vision* 155 🖋 *New Meanings* 156 🖋 *Round Robin* 157 🖋 *Positive Reinforcement* 159 🖋 *Before the Circle* 160 🖋 *Spring Fling* 161 *Untapped Potential* 162 🖋 *Creative Juices* 164 🖋 *Supportive Sisters* 165 🖋 *Caring Friends* 166 🖋 *Apology* 168 🖋 *Apology Accepted* 169 🖋 *Synergy* 170 🖋 *Bank Deposits* 171 🖋 *Inspiration* 172 🖋 *Lydia's Mom's Letter* 173 🖋 *Affirmation* 175 🖋 *Forty Years of Friendship* 176

A B O U T T H E A U T H O R S 177

Lydia Lewis Alexander 178 🖋 *Marilyn Hill Harper* 190 *Otis Holloway Owens* 204 🖋 *Mildred Lucas Patterson* 218

Acknowledgments

This book was based on forty years of friendships; many people contributed to making it a reality.

We are uniquely indebted to our parents for the significant roles they played in shaping our lives through their love, direction, and sacrifices: Flora Laird and Clinton E. Lewis; Eugenia Ashmore and Harold E. Hill; Edna Weiss and Elias Brown Holloway, Jr.; and Lula Smith and James Arthur Lucas.

The husbands, Charles E. Owens and James H. Patterson, Jr., were particularly generous in spending time alone while Otis and Mildred were helping to prepare the manuscript. Otis thanks Charles for the love he has given along the way and his constructive criticism. Mildred thanks James for his love, understanding, suggestions, and support in serving as a sounding board.

Lydia would especially like to acknowledge the continuing support of her mother and mentor, Flora Lewis, and her sister and best friend, Gwendolyn Lewis Harllee.

Otis expresses deep appreciation to her sister, Florence Holloway Perry, for all the joys, sharing, caring, understanding, listening, memories, and laughter in the writing of this book and throughout the years.

Marilyn extends gratitude and love to her sister, Ercelle Hill Pinckney, whose personal choice of caring for their parents allowed Marilyn the freedom to choose her own path; to Angeles Arrien who believed in this book from the beginning; to Claire Blotter who pushed her to open up and write from the soul.

Mildred expresses sincere gratitude to her lifelong friend Annie Mae Belton, for providing her a listening ear; to her brother, Cliston Lucas, for his understanding throughout this process; and to her brother-in-law, Lindsay W. Patterson, for all of his helpful hints as we prepared to go into publication of this book.

Countless friends inspired us as we wrote this book. We wish to express our special thanks to Pinkie Bolden of San Francisco for her true friendship, assistance, and support; our sincere gratitude to Thomas A. Bolden of Jacksonville, Florida, for his friendship and for keeping up with all of us; and our appreciation to Thora L. Dudley of New York City and Bryant Holloway Owens of Charlotte, North Carolina, for their generous expressions of hospitality that made our "editing" trip to New York even more meaningful and exciting.

We are enormously grateful to our editor, Adrienne Ingrum, for her wise guidance and editorial advice and the pleasure of working with her, and our agent, Amy Kossow, of the Linda Allen Literary Agency, for her dedication and commitment throughout this process. We are also appreciative of the professional assistance provided by Jessica Schulte, publisher's associate, and the technical expertise provided by Liana Parry, production editor.

A special thanks to Mary Dekle who prepared the document in its final form, and to Elaine Minter and Vivian McKeever Senior who assisted in the initial drafts. In addition, we sincerely appreciate Dr. Priscilla VanZandt who took the time to critique the organization and structure of the manuscript.

Most especially, we acknowledge the love and support of our sons and our daughters-in-law, the mothers of our future generations: Yolanda Sims and Judson T. Alexander, Jr.; Cathy Summers and Harry D. Harper III; Hill Harper; Maria Marino and Bryant Holloway Owens; Myra Sanders and James H. Patterson III; and Roger Lindsay Patterson.

Introduction

Sorting out midlife transitions is confusing. The four of us are progressing in little steps toward understanding our places in the world at this time of our lives. These letters describe our personal experiences with loss, frustration, self-esteem, and changing life roles. Our relationship with each other emerged as a powerful central theme. In this book we share our happiness about the love and support we receive from each other, as well as our thoughts about midlife issues.

We are African American females, with roots in the Southern United States, who feel our experiences address universal issues. Women face the issues of aging, changing roles of children, and preparing for retirement. The struggle to construct a productive and rewarding life as we proceed toward the so-called golden years is especially difficult in this society, which undervalues both women and elders. Our thoughts, we trust, will be entertaining and helpful.

We seek to inspire women to establish safe circles within which they can discuss personal concerns and discover they are not alone. The challenges of this life cycle are shared by all women, and we can offer each other help, love, and wisdom. Since the four of us live in different parts of the country, our discussions took place via letters, conference calls, and biannual meetings. It is these letters that are compiled into this book. This format made it easier to create and maintain in writing the sense of intimacy we felt during our meetings.

Wearing Purple

A few years ago
Our dresses fit;
Color didn't matter,
With a figure to flatter . . .

Years went by, we became of age;
Our family lives took center stage.

Then—freedom and serenity stalked our minds
As we went adrift in our inner selves.

Now wearing purple from head to toe,
With great beauty to show,
We're enjoying life's treasures,
Inner peace, our letters.

And then, release.

—Mildred Lucas Patterson

PART I

Old, Fat,
and
Forgetful

Marilyn

Dear Lydia,

Although I am still in the midst of the confusion attendant to letting go of old situations and unsure of what direction I will take, I feel calm and happy in the love and support of my sisters.

The letting-go process started ten years ago when I could no longer tolerate my personal living situation. I was with a kind, charming, and reliable man whom I had adored for years. In spite of what had been an almost ideal situation, I grew restless and nearly panic-stricken at the thought of staying there and living out the pattern we had established. There seemed to be no point to it, no challenge in it, and no discernible meaning. I changed home and workplace simultaneously, and have been living the role of seeker ever since. My search has taken me in and out of several relationships and on journeys to Europe and Asia. I have read more than one hundred books covering Buddhism, Taoism, Shamanic traditions, quantum reality, women's issues, and numerous self-help books of the moment. I have attended workshops espousing various methods of dealing with life, tried the occasional church service, and wished it were still the '60s so I could join a commune. The transition is ongoing still. I have found deep meaning in our collective creative activities. I have come to realize how closely we are all related to each other and to nature. I have finally found teachers to help me find my way home.

Until later, much love,
Marilyn

Dear Marilyn,

I enjoyed our chat a few weeks ago about facing "older" age and I think it helped me to feel better about the whole thing. As I told you, when one of my dearest friends (former lover) reminded me that he was "almost sixty," I nearly broke into tears, realizing not only that I, too, am getting closer to sixty than fifty, but also that sixty seems "old" even in my book.

So far, I have managed to elude the matter of age by thinking of myself as "young" and not wanting to be any younger (not even wanting to date younger men). After all, my associates are still considered to be my girlfriends, I still enjoy a lot of things that young people enjoy, and I see a lot of people every day who are apparently a <u>lot</u> older than I am.

Now things are beginning to be different. Now, wrinkled <u>old</u> men say "Yes Ma'am" to me and men have pretty much stopped flirting with me. With my power of rationalization, I will convince myself soon that it isn't my face that looks so old but my extra body weight.

I'll get back to this letter after I start an exercise program. The least I can do is try to <u>feel</u> better; the "looking" better will have to come later.

Love,
Lydia

Lydia

Marilyn

Dear Lydia,

On soft autumn mornings like this one I feel that I'm in just the right place, the time is right, and my mind and body are in harmony that also feels right. For these days, I am immensely grateful. On many other days, I feel old, fat, and forgetful. The physical alterations which beset us during these middle years are sometimes very hard to take. Each alone is quite minor; the combinations become a transition that demands attention.

I had one good year feeling unencumbered by stuff every time I went out. After I stopped smoking I could use tiny, pretty handbags that were lovely accessories rather than utilitarian sacks. Or I could put keys and money in one pocket and a comb and lipstick in the other and go out the door feeling light, moving easily. And then suddenly I can't read a menu or browse through a store checking out the sales without GLASSES! It's back to the big purse. Glasses are really not that big of a deal, except somehow I feel weighted down by them. Guess it's one more peril of getting old.

Love,
Marilyn

Dear Marilyn,

As I reflect on the ways in which I have already noticed significant changes brought on by age, I can easily understand why some people fear the aging process and speak so disparagingly about it. After all, how many women do you know who enjoy being referred to as "ma'am" by little old men who are at least ten years older than they are? I realize some people gray early, but how do you think I feel when someone says, "Is that your natural color or is that really <u>all</u> the gray you have?" (". . . at your age," I figure they want to say.) Believe me, one's potential sexiness can be adversely affected by such unsightly "features" as bulges, a navel buried in a deep sinkhole, lumpy thighs and hips that ring of cellulite at its best, bags under the eyes that resemble miniature pillows, and hands and feet that look dehydrated <u>before</u> they're soaked in water.

As if these effects of aging are not enough, what about the increasing need for eyeglasses to read <u>and</u> to see . . . the likelihood that a hearing aid will be a necessity before long . . . the growing possibility that some type of absorbent pad will become a standard linen item for the bed—to protect you against involuntary loss of bladder control . . . or the need for soundproof body and odor shields to protect you against involuntary expulsion of gas?

One thing is certain. Growing older is far superior to <u>not</u> growing older. If given the choice, I would opt for old age, even with all its drawbacks.

Love,
Lydia

Lydia

Marilyn

16

Dear Lydia,

Middle-age spread is not a myth. I am eating less, exercising regularly—and getting thick in the middle in spite of much effort. It may be necessary to change from walking to running, or try the entirely novel idea of accepting myself as I am. Pinkie and I went to hear Maya Angelou Thursday night and she was wonderful. She recited "Phenomenal Woman" and for a few minutes I felt my size and hair were just fine. I'd like to hold on to that feeling.

An underlying fear exaggerates the importance of getting plump and feeling tired. For me, it is the dread of dependency. The prospect of not being able to care for myself, travel alone, or move my body with grace and flexibility is unnerving. Chances are, none of those will happen. In any event, the real goal is to learn to face all of life's transitions with awareness and compassion.

On the upside, I truly enjoy the perspective on life I have at this time. I have come to trust that problems will get sorted out in good time. I no longer feel that it is necessary to fix everything this very minute. My fiery rage at social injustice has been replaced by a smoldering heat that allows me to respond with a softer strength. I no longer expect racism and sexism to be erased from society. I will also no longer allow an insult to pass without making it clear that such behavior is reprehensible and unacceptable. I now do this with little noise and a large impression.

Love,
Marilyn

Dear Mildred,

WOMAN GIVES BIRTH TO BABY AFTER LIVING ON EARTH FOR MORE THAN A HALF CENTURY.

The headlines glared out of my imagination like the reality of those of the <u>National Enquirer</u>. And again I am drawn face-to-face with understanding my own developmental process.

MENOPAUSE—i.e., the period of natural cessation of menstruation occurring usually between the ages of forty-five and fifty.

I never expected that I would be traumatized by the experience of menopause. And yet the "M" word now looms large in my consciousness as I remain in anticipation of the ending of a ritual which now spans some forty-five years of my life. I am beginning to question if having a menstrual cycle will ever finally be over.

I really don't know how to anticipate the age when I was likely to stop menstruating. Well, I have had my last period for well over two years now. That is, I think it's my last period each time. There has definitely been a change in the pattern of my periods. The time between periods has progressed from a few extra days to sixty days and more recently to six months. I think I will make an appointment with the doctor today to make sure that the delay in this stage is, in fact, natural. Physically and mentally, I am feeling quite well and seem more energetic than I have been for years. Who knows what is causing the slow-down of this passage?

Love,

Otis

Marilyn

18

Dear Lydia,

Do you remember Judith from Atlanta? She visited last week and I was upset by her views on getting older. She said, "No man wants a 52-year-old woman." I was shocked at her assessment of herself, and thus of me, as undesirable. Since that evening I've carefully noticed various pairs, checking out which women of a certain age were alone, which in clearly long-standing relationships, which seemed to be with a new man. Judith was wrong. Women with energy and vitality still attract male attention. Some of the women seem complete and radiant either in a pair or alone. I have concluded that the mystery of sexual attraction relates so much to the essential nature of each party that age alone must play a small part. It may be that all the attention to hair and makeup and clothes is as much in the service of pleasing ourselves with our image as it is designed to attract.

On balance, this age is just okay with me.

Take care.

Love,
Marilyn

Dear Marilyn,

Did I suggest that we comment on sexuality? I can't imagine how valuable words on such a subject might be from one who isn't sexually active. "Sexually inactive" women need to know how to survive in a time when sex seems uppermost in most people's minds.

For me, a sexual experience is a feeling of gratification that can be brought on by stimulation other than with the clitoris. I find myself excited when I'm in the presence of someone who makes me feel loved. The mere touch of someone whose love emanates from a smile, a warm look, or a gentle word. For me, a stimulating conversation can cause excitement that can be so rejuvenating that I can reach a special kind of orgasm with little or no effort. It's a shame my friend never knew how little it would take to satisfy me after an evening of his conversation and gentle touching.

What do I do about sex now? Nothing. I handle it just as I handle misery—I stay busy and try not to think about it. Strangely enough, I don't think I'm really missing much—maybe because I never considered myself highly sexed—but I would not turn down an exciting opportunity to be proven wrong.

Love,
Lydia

Lydia

Marilyn

Dear Lydia,

My love life is suffering. I met an anesthesiologist at a meeting this summer and he's been to visit once. He seems nice and I hope he'll be a good traveling companion. I'm not in love with him. In fact, I've given up on falling in love and only hope for good companionship. Isn't that something? Such a switch and so boring!! Sounds safe, though. I try to imagine what it would be like to live in Minnesota, but the images are fuzzy. The long winters would probably drive me to suicide in a few weeks.

All's well with the boys and my folks. Frank is having quite a time with first-year law at Harvard. I read that book about Harvard called <u>One L</u> and it sounded terrible. He's a survivor though, so I'm not worried. Harry and family come down for the weekend occasionally. I truly enjoy little Tory. It makes me wonder what it would be like to have a daughter, something you and I won't experience.

My Halloween party was a big success. At least everyone seemed to have a good time. I was a little less thrilled than usual. I think this will be the last one. I've had it for several years and I think its time has passed. Now it's time for something else or maybe nothing for a while.

Take good care of yourself during the Christmas chaos.

Love,
Marilyn

Dear Otis,

Your letter about the effects of menopause on the developing woman made me wonder what I might have missed as a result of my surgical menopause in 1984. While I had only a week or two to reflect on the decision regarding the surgery, it seemed clear that the benefits far outweighed the disadvantages. After all, I did not want to have any more children, and removal of both the uterus and ovaries would eliminate the possibility of cervical and ovarian cancer. Of course, if I had listened to my great-aunt, I might not have agreed to surgery. "I think it's very important for a woman to please her husband in bed, and one thing men like is feeling a 'grip' when they're having sex with a woman," she said to me. When I told her that the doctor said there would be no difference the man could detect, she said, "Common sense will tell you that if everything is taken out, there won't be anything left up there to 'grip' him with."

It seemed the women who had the greatest fears of a hysterectomy had never had the surgery, while women who had undergone the surgery were generally positive about it. The most positive response was from my cousin who said, "I was afraid I wouldn't 'get wet' during sex after my body no longer produced hormones, but with hormone therapy, I get as wet as I ever did and I enjoy sex so much more because I am free of the fear of getting pregnant."

My instant leap into menopause was one of the best things that ever happened to me. I continued to enjoy sex—I certainly enjoyed being free of the burden of possible pregnancy—I was no longer inconvenienced by the extra baggage that I carried around during those special days each month, and I never again experienced that pain that had been known to take me to my knees. By the time I had grown accustomed to enjoying sex without such paraphernalia as diaphragms, gels, condoms, and foams, the threat of AIDS made it necessary to start packing the bags again. Now I wonder if sex is worth all of the trouble unless, of course, you can limit your activity to the seldom-found "loyal" mate.

I don't normally have hot flashes, but writing about menopause has suddenly caused me to sweat.

Love,
Lydia

Lydia

Dear Otis,

What a difference a day makes! I remember so vividly when I was young, thin, and attractive. As a matter of fact, I felt real good. Some days now I look in the mirror and say, "Mirror, mirror on the wall— this body of mine has had a great fall." Then I wonder, "What am I going to do about it?" Those are the days when I wake up bloated with gas, and have eyelids that are as puffed as balloons. The more I work on my physical self, the more depressed I seem to become. Nothing I see or do seems to go quite right for me on those rare days. I seem to get out of bed with a "Geritol" feeling, and a difficult attitude. Television drives me crazy and talk radio puts me to sleep. I count my calories and still gain weight just looking at food; flush my digestive system with roughage and still become constipated; buy every advertised skin product that I can afford and I still get dry, cracked skin with a few wrinkles here and there. Friends a few years younger tell me that they want to look like me when they get older—and I think that they look like me now. So on those real "bad" days, I like to go into hiding with only <u>myself</u>. But yesterday was different. When the menopause blues attacked, I decided to counteract it with a different strategy. I retreated to my backyard to enjoy the singing birds and help Pat (my honeydew) install a flower garden. As I began to work, I observed that the birds no longer enjoyed my "old" bird feeder. They seemed to be hanging out in my neighbor's yard. At that moment, I dashed to the store and returned with a bird feeder that was fit for a queen. This compulsive buying was totally out of character for me. I was now discovering who I had

Mildred

23

become, and I began to feel menopause behavior unfold before my eyes. Now I realize that sometimes it has been very difficult for me to live with myself, so I know that I have created some difficult times for others. I will stop at this moment to apologize to the world: "Sorry world! Thanks for loving me in spite of myself."

Two days have passed since our garden project began. With continuous teamwork, we have turned our backyard into a thing of beauty. Not only is it a sanctuary for the birds, but it also provides a sanctuary for the two of us. Now, in the warm evenings, instead of concentrating on the things I cannot change, Pat and I retreat to our backyard to forget the city noises. He reads his newspaper, and fills me in on the last days of his job. His retirement is fast approaching. He is counting the days. For the first time in thirty-four years, I am a good listener. We have declared quiet time for ourselves. What a good feeling! This makes senior citizen status more meaningful and menopause less stressful.

It's 10:00 P.M.—long past my bedtime. That's another complaint I have—The older I get, the more sleep I need. (Smiles.)

See you.

Love,

Mildred

Mildred

24

Dear Lydia,

I remember on one visit Otis asking questions about menopause and it was such a great release. I was delighted to just talk about what was happening even though, as I recall, we spoke mainly of the physical aspects of menopause. For a long time I felt I'd be one of those women who would have a late-life child. Heaven knows that I can't imagine raising a little one now; the noise alone would drive me crazy. Yet I still feel the lost option of bearing children as a sadness. It feels like the gifts I can offer my loved ones are significantly different—perhaps more valuable, but definitely different. The fact that we share this life transition and talk about it is wonderful.

Love,
Marilyn

Marilyn

25

Dear Otis,

Ten years ago, when I was forty-eight years old and a close friend was fifty-eight years old, I received a telephone call one dreary night and she began to sing in her contralto voice, "Nobody knows the trouble I've seen, nobody knows but Jesus." Her voice began to fade into tears and she began to pour her heart out to me and tell me about her ups and downs.

At that time in my life, I was still vivacious and had just experienced a late-life miscarriage. She was into menopause and I was a great listener, but I really didn't know what she was experiencing.

This friend whom I had known for many years was always the one whom everyone turned to when they had a problem. She was a great counselor and confidante, a great listener. She shared my pleasure in the best of times and offered me comfort in the worst of times. Her advice was always well taken. Now she needed a listening ear. Even though she has many friends, she chose my shoulder to lean on. "It's my turn," I said. She talked nonstop about her painful "down" moments and her sometimes "up" moments. She began to relate incidents that were bothering her but that ten years prior were too trivial to discuss. When she finished hashing and rehashing, she remarked how comforting it was to talk and feel safe talking, having neither to weigh her thoughts nor measure her words. She just poured her problems out, knowing that a faithful friend was on the other end waiting to sift through her conversation, listen, and provide a shoulder of kindness and comfort.

I called her one day recently when I was stressed out over an unpleasant incident in my life, and I began to sing, "Nobody knows the trouble I've seen, nobody knows but Jesus." This old spiritual was being sung with new meaning for me. My friend chuckled and said, "Start talking. I've been there."

Love,
Mildred

Mildred

Marilyn

Dear Lydia,

When you asked me how I handle frustration, my mind went blank. I know that sick stomach, sinking pain, and bile taste that tell me frustration is back again, but what exactly is it? My old dictionary gives me the first definition as "to make plans worthless or of no avail." So the question becomes, what do I do when I'm thwarted or blocked or forced to admit defeat? First I cry, then I try again.

Now I am trying to avoid putting a high value on my plans. If I am not too attached to the end result, I'm less likely to feel frustration. Over the years, I've been told in numerous different ways to live for today, to do what's right for right's own sake, to study for the beauty of knowledge, not for grades. I think all these old adages amount to much the same thing: do what you do because you love doing it, not for the sake of results. Learning to focus on the <u>doing</u> is difficult, but it brings great rewards.

Another frustrating area that I have not relinquished is the search for a life partner. I have not met this mythical person and may not recognize him if he walks in the front door. My plan to have a partner on this life's journey has come to nothing. I am close to letting go of that hope, but not there yet. Take care.

Much love,

Marilyn

Dear Mildred,

"Are you poor, Aunt Jemima? Are you poor, Aunt Jemima?"

The words rang clear! I looked up from my charcoal grill and the two Omaha filet mignon steaks grilling to perfection. Both the steaks and the grilling were special in celebration of our 25th wedding anniversary. The moment was tranquil and almost magical. I was feeling especially peaceful, at home among the trees, azaleas, singing birds, and squirrels swinging from branch to branch.

"Are you poor, Aunt Jemima? Are you poor, Aunt Jemima?"

The words seemed surreal. I looked up and faced two five-year-old white boys in the distance continuing to chant—"Are you poor, Aunt Jemima?"

My earlier feeling of peace and tranquility quickly turned to anger and frustration. The words pierced my inner peace, attacked my psyche, my history, my space. The children shouted the question again, "Are you poor, Aunt Jemima?" Almost without thinking, I shouted, "Do your parents know what you are saying?"

My frustration heightened as I went inside the house to tell Charles how I had been victimized in my own backyard. Realizing the intensity of my anger, Charles suggested that he would go over and talk with the father later. There was a knock at the door. I knew immediately, even though I had never seen the man, that he must be the parent of the boys who were taunting me earlier. He said that he had heard the boys making insulting comments to me earlier and he wanted to assure us that he and his wife disapproved

Otis

29

of the boys' inappropriate behavior. Further, he noted that he had talked with the boys about what they had done. The father seemed so genuinely apologetic that some of my raw anger was disarmed. And now I am left with a growing sense of frustration.

Somehow I guess this incident simply put me on notice that there is much yet to be done before blacks in America can enjoy, with dignity, a society without stereotypes, discrimination, or other injustices. Perhaps this was my wake-up call to the reality that we are not yet assured of a comfortable place in this society.

I thought that at this stage of my life I would have the luxury of concentrating on the more normal frustrations of life, such as menopause, arthritis, high blood pressure, trying to remember important names and dates, and retirement plans. Have I been living in a fantasy world? I had experienced the indignities of living in this society, in my home in the suburbs, a "nice" upper-middle-class neighborhood. These two five-year-old white boys might not realize the full implication of their quest to determine if Aunt Jemima is poor. Yes, Aunt Jemima is poor and rich, educated and ignorant, nice and not so nice. In the eyes of America she continues to exist in places where we least expect to find her, <u>like in your own backyard</u>.

Love,

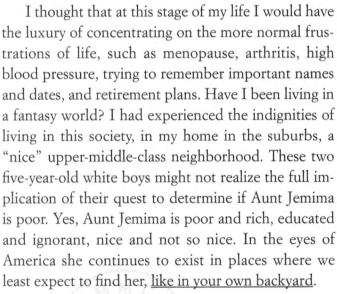

Otis

30

Dear Otis,

I have been at this shop for two hours waiting for my tires to be repaired, and I have had to bite my tongue to control my frustrations. I feel that I could be using this time to pack my clothes for San Francisco. The manager continues to come in the waiting room to give me bad news on the demise of my tires. At one point in my life, this kind of news did not faze me. But as I prepare for retirement, I want to put a Band-Aid on car problems and other problems facing me.

This letter enables me to vent some frustration that has mounted up for several months. I sure would like to find another type of employment, probably become self-employed. I am working toward that end and exploring my options. I have explored day care, small business (maybe a boutique since I enjoy putting fashions together), writing, and opening a flea market or resale shop. Whatever the case, I would like to supplement my retirement. I am too young to begin my Social Security and too old to want to work full-time. I am in a dilemma.

Thanks to you and my dear friends Lydia and Marilyn, I can vent, get some relief, and return to the same job with a new lease on life. Thanks for lending me your ear. I feel better already.

Love,
Mildred

Mildred

Dear Mildred,

Charles and I drove to Birmingham to visit family feeling confident that Bryant (then eighteen years old) would act responsibly. Prior to leaving on our trip we talked with Bryant regarding our expectations for his behavior. It was the first time we left him alone. We specifically said, "No girls or boys in the house while we are away. PERIOD."

The telephone rang and it was for me. My neighbor Carolyn Ballou, in a calm voice, said, "Otis, I think there is a party going on at your house."

I said, "Hang on I will get right back to you."

Ringgggggggggggggg. "Hello, son."

"Hi, Mom."

"I just spoke with Mrs. Ballou and she told me that there is a party going on at my house."

"Oh, no, Mom, it's just a couple of my friends who stopped by to pick me up. We are going to the movies."

"Well, son, you know the rules. Nobody, except you, in the house while we are gone."

"Okay, Mom. We are on our way out."

"Hi, Carolyn, I just spoke with Bryant and he said that a couple of his friends had just stopped by and they are on their way to the movies."

"Well, that's very interesting. There might be only one or two people there but they came in fifteen or twenty cars."

"What? I'll call you right back."

Ringgggggggggggggggg. "BRYANT, Mrs. Ballou said that your two friends arrived in fifteen or twenty cars. GET THEM OUT! And get them out NOW. You have two minutes. I am calling Mr. Ballou to come down there and make sure that all of those people are out and that you are home. He will be instructed to call the police to arrest everybody, including you, if they are not out when he gets there." I felt confident that Mr. Ballou would make the proper assessment since he was formerly a policeman.

Mildred, I can't begin to tell you just how many telephone calls we made between Birmingham and Jacksonville, Florida, that weekend.

I learned from my nephew Bertram in Birmingham that he and Bryant also made numerous telephone calls that weekend. He said Bryant seemed unconcerned at first and then wanted to know "Just how mad are my parents?" Bertram warned him that we must be pretty upset because we had cut our trip short and left Birmingham at six o'clock in the morning to drive back to Jacksonville.

33

Once home, we had to mete out the strictest discipline ever to help Bryant understand the consequences of betraying our trust. First we talked. Charles is a master of delivering disciplinary discourse. In addition, we imposed extensive denial of privileges including driving the car and going places other than to school and church. Never trust an eighteen-year-old.

Love,
Otis

Lydia

Dear Marilyn,

How do I deal with frustration? One technique that I use is "talking it out" with a friend or family member. In most cases, I use my sister as a sounding board. For many other things, I use my mother. Other valuable tools that I use in dealing with frustration are my sense of humor and my candor in dealing with people. I laugh a lot—at myself as well as with others—and I believe that the laughing helps me to maintain some semblance of sanity.

In my young, more daring days, I would grab a drink or two, and one cigarette after another to ease my frustrations. In some strange way, I was fooling myself into believing that I was getting relief from a pressing problem. When I freed myself of those habits, I realized that they didn't help; they just tended to make me put off dealing with the problem.

Ultimately, I rely on divine guidance. I still have difficulty turning problems over to the Lord completely, probably because I feel such a need to do all He has empowered me to do before I admit that I can't do any more. If it were not for my sister, my mother, and a few special friends—like you, Otis, and Mildred—I don't know what I'd do. I'm really looking forward to seeing all of you in San Francisco. The setting and atmosphere there go a long way toward helping me deal with frustration.

Love,

Lydia

Dear Otis,

You asked if I am able to vent frustrations? In answering, I will say "I try to avoid stressful days. Sometimes, my temperament runs hot and cold." I am not naive to think that I will have all good days and all victories, but I would like to aim my life toward a certain comfort level with minimum frustration and maximum joy. Therefore, I have learned to cope with frustration by engaging my mind in certain activities. I am going to share some of these activities with you. I must admit that sometimes I don't practice what I preach, so that old "frustration bug" just sneaks up on me. However, I enjoy making a calendar of events to have handy when I need to vent some frustrations. So I:

Mildred

> Keep friends on call who enjoy eating out on short notice.
> Keep Scrabble, card, and Bingo buddies available.
> Weave fun out of "shopping till I drop."
> Take nature walks and meditate.
> Use my hands to create.
> Keep up with sorority activities and stay involved with youth-oriented projects.
> Give time and attention to church-related activities.

Otis, I stay very busy interacting with others. Therefore, I vent my frustrations in a variety of activities.

Sometimes I become frustrated when I think about retirement. At this writing, I am exploring my options. I will keep you updated as my decision unfolds.

Love, Mildred

Mildred

Dear Lydia,

I am compelled to write this letter because you are playing a similar role as caregiver as I did from 1975 to 1978. Each time I inquire about your mother's health, I reflect on my mother's illness.

I remember how strong and courageous my mother was throughout her unexpected illness. We had never seen her encounter an illness—not even a toothache. My dad, who died in 1974 at the age of eighty-two, was the one with perpetual complaints. When Dad died, Mom never released him emotionally. She never cried. Six months after his death, I saw a frail, weakened Mom who began to complain about pain under her rib cage. I tried to coax her into getting a complete physical examination, but she assured me that it was only a little indigestion. I worried about her health, but didn't pay it much attention because she had never been ill before.

Six months later, I received the unexpected news that Mom had been diagnosed with multiple myeloma (cancer of the bone marrow). I was not familiar with that form of cancer, but I was aware that any form of cancer was serious. I cried my heart out as I prepared to go to my mom's bedside to become the "rock" in the family. I remembered praying that God would give me the strength to make the best decisions about Mama's health care.

During the three years that I was Mama's caregiver, many changes took place in our lives. I was there for her good days and her very sick days. For the first time we had uninterrupted quality time. May God continue to give you strength.

Love, *Mildred*

Dear Mildred,

Thanks for your words of encouragement. The life of a caregiver has many ups and downs, but we can never survive the "downs" if we don't believe the "ups" make them all worthwhile. While I do what I can for my physically challenged mother, it can only loosely be defined as caregiving.

I see her briefly each morning when I take her breakfast. I call her periodically during the day; I see her briefly in the evening when I stop by after leaving work. Except for out-of-town trips that we take together, I don't spend a lot of time with her, nor am I responsible for her care. The nursing care that she receives—the bathing, the changing, the dressing—now that's true caregiving. If I had all of that to do, I would have a different story to tell.

God knows I don't mind doing for my mother what she can't do—or what is difficult for her to do—like running errands and retrieving objects that she can't reach. But I do mind her asking me to do things that she still has the strength and ability to do herself. I get so frustrated when she asks me to "think" for her or to "write" something for her, because her mind is as sharp as it can be. It irritates me for her to ask me to "call" someone for her or to "shop around" for something that she needs when it will take little effort on her part to make her own telephone calls and do her own Yellow Pages shopping in the comfort of her chair.

We do what we have to do in this life, and I feel the need to do whatever I can for my mom. I'm basically all that she has at home (in terms of family) and I know if the situation were reversed, she

Lydia

UPS AND DOWNS

37

would do even more for me. Even now, she frequently asks what she can do to help me during times that I am busiest.

I can only hope that if fate should have it that I might become physically challenged someday like my mom is now, that my son will be equally attentive to my needs.

Love,
Lydia

Lydia

Dear Mildred,

You are so very lucky. It sounds like caring for your mother for those last three years was a blessing rather than a problem. It is truly a gift to have a positive and uplifting experience during those difficult days. I have several friends who are not so lucky. They are being squeezed financially and emotionally by parental demands. It is heart-wrenching sometimes to be committed to what one considered the right thing to do and have fewer and fewer resources to accomplish the task.

My sister has assumed responsibility for my mother. Many years ago when I tried to talk Ercelle into coming to California, she said she needed to stay in South Carolina for our parents, and she's done just that. I think it has become more restricting than she imagined. It is hard for me to help very much. I try to be supportive but my comments fall flat. After all, I have the freedom to come and go as I please without arranging for a "baby-sitter." Ercelle does not complain and she is doing a fabulous job.

Mother's hearing is failing and she cannot handle the telephone well, which means that the long telephone talks we used to have are a thing of the past. We are getting a headset-style phone for her which may help. Her stroke left her right side virtually useless, so cooking and tending to her plants, which were her favorite activities, are now impossible. She remains pleasant and patient and laughs easily. I hold Mother in my meditations and hope this is enough.

Love,
Marilyn

Marilyn

39

Dear Lydia,

I am happy that your mother is recovering so well after her latest hospitalization. It is truly amazing how she is able to mobilize in her wheelchair. I am sure that the fact that she is in her "own" house is a vital ingredient in her recuperation. I admire your ability to maintain your busy work schedule, attend to your civic and organizational commitments, and still find both the time and energy to prepare breakfast for your mom and to visit with her in the evening. I recall that you said you do not consider yourself to be your mom's caregiver. I know that she is pleased to have you do some of the things for her that she cannot do for herself.

Attending to a parent's physical needs can be emotionally taxing. But the special kind of relationship you and your mom seem to enjoy has made a situation that could be exceptionally taxing an experience that is especially meaningful. She must really enjoy your daily visits. After all, you are an engaging conversationalist, a creative humorist, and a skillful game player. You both have such positive attitudes and we all know that a positive attitude is an essential ingredient in living life to the fullest.

It is important that we be allowed (and allow others, including our parents or children) to maintain a sense of independence, dignity, and pride.

I learned an important lesson when Mamma experienced what we now believe was her first neurological problem. After she had been evaluated by Tuscaloosa's best physician, Florence and I met with him to discuss his prognosis of the problem and to inform him that he had to tell Mamma she could no longer live alone. After rolling his eyes heavenward he said, "Leave her alone! Let her live in her own house for as long as she wants to do so." Then he enumerated example after example of his patients (who seemed in much worse condition than Mamma was at the time) who were living on their own, alone. Well, Mamma lived alone for years before we determined that it was no longer safe for her to do so.

As you know, Florence was Mamma's chief caregiver. I have a deep feeling of gratitude for the care she gave to Mamma while she was in nursing homes in Birmingham. Florence visited Mamma almost every day. I know there were days when she was physically exhausted, yet she found the energy to go to the nursing home, visit Mamma, pick up dirty laundry, and wash clothes before she could even relax after working all day. This only describes the logistical care. I cannot begin to describe the constant care and concern of an emotional nature.

Otis

41

Fortunately, though maybe frustrating for you, your mom is extremely capable of making her own decisions. I don't think any of us is ever prepared for the role reversal when we must become guardians of our parents. You know well that caring for a parent is even more demanding than caring for a child.

I hope that you are taking care of yourself in the process. Remember, I am here if you ever need to talk.

Love,

Otis

Dear Marilyn,

How could anyone think that we don't have our moments of misery, loneliness, and despair? Everyone does! I know I've had my share of misery, but I always manage to spring back. I can't imagine how people without faith ever manage to cope, not just with adversity but also with success. Reflecting on some of my most miserable moments makes me realize the importance of being guided by a spiritual force outside of myself. Without the Lord to ease my pain and dry my tears, I don't know what I'd do or be.

How do I deal with my misery? I don't. I try not to think about it. When I'm forced to think about it, I laugh at myself. Thank God I have a sense of humor. Without it, I'd be dead! When I'm not laughing, I cry sometimes when I'm alone . . . just like I did during Christmas when the Brady Bunch family reunion reminded me of how awful it is to be alone at Christmas. Everybody needs somebody to love. Even though I know I'm too busy to be a good wife, and I would be miserable as a wife with nothing else to do besides drown in domestic duties, I can't pass a smiling couple without wishing that I could revive that part of my life that was not so empty. I can't help wishing for the days that I could snuggle up to J.T. in a movie, cuddle beside him in bed at night (whether I wanted to have sex or not), fuss with him over spending money, or bicker over who would do the household chores. How I long for those moments I used to dread!! Now, simple things like attending parties, banquets, and social events where couples abound have become drudgery for me—even the few minutes required to make an obligatory appearance. When I have the greatest success in rationalizing, it's when I remind myself that having someone could be worse. It's unlikely that I'll be lucky enough to find another man as secure in himself as J.T. was, or as supportive of my efforts to "be involved," so I pause and count my blessings. Believe it or not, the misery I'm experiencing now seems superior to most of the alternatives that come to mind.

Isn't it a good thing I have so much to think about and do? Pausing too long to ponder your misery can be depressing.

Pray for me,
Lydia

Lydia

Mildred

Dear Lydia,

I tensed up as I read your comments on misery. You have always been the fun person who taught me to turn some of my negative reactions into jokes, even though I might cry inside afterward. Just as I was taking a page out of your "book" of emotional stability, I read your letter as you related some feelings of misery. I felt that I would like to respond.

I want to share a few of my down moments and how I coped with them. Christmas has been a sad time since my mother's death. One of the ways I have learned to reduce stress is by sharing with the needy. When our sons were ten and fourteen years old, Pat and I donated four hours to feeding the homeless on Christmas Day. This was done after we exchanged our family gifts under the Christmas tree. We also shared our Christmas gifts with them.

Christmas of 1994, James III and his family were unable to make the drive from Minnesota to North Carolina to celebrate the holidays with us. I had to let my creative juices flow. We celebrated the "Twelve Days of Christmas." We mailed love gifts to our grandchildren for twelve days—books, stuffed toys, pictures of their father and uncle in their youth, a family picture for their photo album, coloring books, Kwanzaa activities with the seven principles, an African American handmade Santa with directions and materials for making their own. I think the grandkids were more excited than they would have been had they visited us, and I had fun doing it. So Lydia, when we dare to be depressed, we need only to remember how blessed we really are and how creative we can be.

Love, *Mildred*

My dear Mildred and Lydia,

I read your letters with great interest since you discussed issues that hold great concern for me. On a personal level, I too, just as most human beings, have experienced feelings of sadness and misery. Fortunately, I have been surrounded by two masters at coping with adversity: first, my mother, who exemplified the tenets of the power of positive thinking, and now by Charles, who seemingly was born devoid of a "poor me" gene. His standard operating procedure (SOP) when he or I hit the wall of confusion or misery is to ask the question, "What can we do to change or cope with the situation?"

Throughout my lifetime I have experienced the blues associated with the physical dynamics of my body. Anxiety and depressed feelings occurred a few days just prior to my monthly menstrual period. What a relief it was for my period to begin flowing. At another time I suffered the wrath of a boss who seemed both unprepared and unaware of certain pressures placed on me. On a daily basis, I considered leaving the job. Charles reminded me that if things were that bad, "then leave, we can make it without your job." He also encouraged me to say exactly what I wanted to say to the boss. I used my usual coping skill of prayer and actually prayed that the Lord would remove that person from my daily life. My prayers were answered. Coping with misery and sadness daily is challenging. I continue to seek wisdom on this issue. Thank you for listening.

Love,

Otis

Mildred

___

Dear Otis,

Pat has been retired fifteen days now. I don't think he believes that he has retired because he promised me that as soon as he retired he would clean out the very congested basement filled with throwaway treasures that span a total of thirty years. He has not begun this task yet. This is one reason I was anticipating his retirement.

In spite of the unfinished basement cleaning, Pat has been rejuvenated in just fifteen days. His skin tone is more youthful. He has more pep to his step, and the occasional snoring has improved. He is finding precious time for himself. Pat's job was a seven-day-a-week job because of his total commitment. The rest of his time was spent taking care of family needs. He deserves retirement.

Pat and our dog, Ash, are now spending many days together. They jog together and enjoy each other's company. Ash, who used to follow me around the house, is now following Pat, the man of leisure. It's quite a treat to observe Ash's reversed behavior.

I suggested that Pat get a part-time job. He looked at me with disdain and replied that he had paid his dues to society. He gave it his best years and his last years will be declared for James and family. I smiled secretly and said, "You go, Pat." Even though I would like to interest him in a part-time job, I respect a man who makes a decision and sticks by it.

Love,
Mildred

Dear Lydia,

What's going on with you? It'll be good to speak with everyone Sunday. I am grappling with decisions about the house in Sebastopol and really need some advice. Yesterday Mr. McIntyre brought by plans for remodeling the house. You know how I've been whining for years about how much I want to retire from medicine, move to the country, write full-time, read all those books I have stacked up, garden a little, play a lot. Those dreams have suddenly moved from misty, distant fantasies to bright, stark possibilities. I have to make real decisions. I have to consider a real commitment to a new lifestyle.

Am I ready to move to a small town alone? Do I want a partner for this time in my life? Will I have more fun designing the house and deciding on stuff like toilets alone or with another? Will it be too quiet on Alta Lane when I'm there full-time? Can I really afford to remodel? Is that the best use of my resources? Would it be better to look for a new house instead of remodeling?

I want to write, but does anyone want to read what I produce? I want peace and quiet, but will I be satisfied not talking to anyone in person for days on end? I want community, but will I find a compatible circle in Sebastopol? I want to leave the hospital hassle, but will I miss the excitement of a difficult case done well? I want to give up the practice of anesthesia, but am I attached to the energy surge associated with caring for critically ill patients? I want to see fresh veggies grow, but do I have the patience to weed and water? I want to live in the trees, but will I miss too severely the fun times in the city? I love the

Marilyn

47

quiet little lane, but do I want to live there forever? Why do these decisions feel so final? Why isn't it okay for them to be final? Am I afraid that after I make this move I will not have the time, energy, or resources to change again? Why do I always need a way out? Why can't I commit to being in one place with one person, come what may? How can I hold the wants and fears in balance? When will I relax and trust myself to manifest the best plan for my life?

It feels so good to say these things to you. I await your opinions. Write soon.

Take care, love,
Marilyn

Marilyn

PART II

Letting Go

Marilyn

Dear Lydia,

I am learning to regard loss as a process of letting go. It's a lovely concept which views loss as a type of transformation, of growth. This is difficult, as you can well imagine. I may not get it learned in this lifetime.

My greatest loss was not my own. When Harry had the BB gun accident and lost his right eye, I felt unbelievable pain. He lost an eye, I lost my firstborn. He became a different child, less energetic, less interested, unsure of his direction, easy prey to adolescent distractions. Fifteen years later, he has only recently appeared somewhat content and finally confident. I was living with Rod at the time. He is a type most clearly described as a rock. (We dingbat types need rocks!) He simply stood still, unwavering, while I raged in anger, grief, and despair. He reminded me of Otis with her quality of constancy. Last summer when Daddy died, she was there, dependable, caring, and willing to sit with me. Her presence and words of comfort and advice were immensely valuable and greatly appreciated.

Love,
Marilyn

Dear Mildred,

We all share some of the losses Marilyn shared with us in her letter. But I guess the most profound losses for me have centered around people. The death of my dad was a loss so significant that it merits another letter.

Then there were and are missed opportunities. If only I could remember what they were—maybe it was a chance to listen to a bird sing when getting to work or doing work seemed more important . . . or maybe it was not taking the time to talk to a stranger . . . or perhaps it was not taking a chance on life . . . or was it missing the boat?—I don't know what boat. I know that losses can be profound though they may seem minor. In the spiritual sense, losses can be present opportunities, as in the Christian reality that Good Friday (i.e., death) offered the opportunity for the Resurrection (i.e., everlasting life).

I have shared some of your losses through the years and you have shared some of mine. Having sensitive, caring friends is a special experience.

Love,
Otis

Otis

Dear Marilyn,

As Easter approaches I am reminded of the pain associated with death and the importance of remembering resurrection and rebirth. In order that I might offset the pain of loss through death, I thought that I would balance my losses with the "gains" that accompanied them. I believe that all things work together for good for those who love the Lord and that out of every (even bad) experience, some good emerges.

The most devastating of the losses that I have experienced are the deaths of my father and my husband, both of which were sudden and quite unexpected. Daddy and J.T. were both so important in my life that I sometimes still have difficulty believing that I am managing without them. I suppose they both spoiled me in a way by allowing me to lean on them for advice, support, and motivation. I learned, increasingly with each of their deaths, the importance of independence and intrinsic motivation for survival. I had relied on them far too much for my own well being.

I still miss Daddy and J.T. a lot, particularly when I am basking in the joy brought on by my grandson. I can imagine how much J.T. would have enjoyed Theo, and in reflecting on the relationship that Judson had with my father, I can imagine that Daddy would have enjoyed his great-grandson even more. When I think of how blessed I am to have had Daddy and J.T. for the time that I did, I smile. Some people <u>never</u> experience such relationships.

Love,
Lydia

Dear Otis,

When I was seven years old, I experienced a great loss. Life was moving along smoothly, I had no worries because I had a big sister, Veen, a senior in college who acted like a second mother to me. My mother was a working mother and it seemed that Veen was always there with a smile. She always told me that "a smile costs nothing, but gives much." I believed in Veen and I was enriched by her many smiles, even when she disciplined me. After the crying and anger, I always remembered to smile, for she had taught me that a smile could bring sunshine to the sad and it was nature's best antidote for trouble. She taught me to believe that I could be anything and do anything I chose to do. She was such a giving person, a caregiver in the truest sense of the word.

One of the saddest days of my life was Veen's sudden illness and her subsequent death. The doctors were not able to diagnose her condition. My mother struggled long and hard to save her first-born child, as I stood helplessly wishing for a miracle. Her illness won out—her death hit me like an avalanche. Since then I was determined to live out Veen's dream to graduate from college.

Love,
Mildred

Mildred

53

Dear Marilyn,

When J.T. died from a tragic accident in 1980, I thought that my world had again come to an end. Daddy's death had removed one of my crutches, then J.T.'s death took the other one away. I couldn't imagine facing life alone, being mom and dad to our son, who had just enrolled for his freshman year at Talladega, and providing moral support for my mother (who was experiencing physical problems related to her legs and back), as well as for other members of my extended family.

J.T. had been my biggest fan, my principal motivator, the primary source of my common sense, and the kind of husband and father that many women wish they had. The two characteristics that separated him from most men were his security in himself and his abundance of sense. I realized how special these traits were when I tried to find them in someone else.

Love,
Lydia

Lydia

My dear Mildred,

On April 28th my mother celebrated her 84th birthday. Since Mamma can't speak to me any longer by phone, I usually call Florence to celebrate Mamma's special day, and Florence and I reminisce about something amusing or amazing. I realized what a painful sense of loss I feel since Mamma has been in the nursing home. The feeling is almost indescribable. She has been transformed from the Mamma I knew. Once vibrant, active, caring, sweet, thoughtful, generous, sensitive, and intelligent, she is now inactive and unable to think or talk.

On her birthday, I felt even sadder when Florence told me that Mamma was not included in the resident birthday party for the third year. Earlier in the month, Florence had served notice to the activities director that she DID NOT want Mamma to miss the party again this year. Florence and I felt hurt and disappointed and angry that Mamma was not treated as the special person that she is. While she may not be responsive, we consider it important for her to be included in the activities that she can attend. At another time, Mamma would have been the person to organize the party, to plan the events, activities, and food for the entire group. She loved celebrations and enjoyed doing things for others.

Love,
Otis

Otis

Otis

Dear Mildred,

Mamma's condition continues to weigh heavily on my heart. Though Mamma may be trapped in her own mind and unable to express herself except on rare occasions, she does have some understanding of things and people around her. I know that God has a purpose for her life—something more than just integrating the nursing homes in Birmingham. Perhaps the purpose of her life is to help others, including me, to ponder the meaning of life and to discover the continuity of the human spirit. I pray for wisdom and understanding—Lord, what would you have me do?

Not only was Mamma lost to me but she was lost to herself. When she was still talking she would ask, "Who are my people? Who am I?" She didn't know who she was and neither did I. But I wrote the following poem in an effort to answer the question.

Who Am I?

You are a strong snow-capped mountain of
*   granite,*
A giant oak tree transplanted from a small town
*   to the inner city,*
A fragile bird sailing in the wind without
*   radar—*
My mother whom the years have transformed.
                              —Otis Holloway Owens, 1988

Thank you for being my sounding board and my friend.

                                        Love,
                                        Otis

Dear Otis and Florence,

After the telephone call last night informing Marilyn and me about the death of your mother yesterday, I paused to say a prayer for your mother, one of my heroes in life. I reflected on my Talladega College years when I needed friends as I adjusted to a new environment. Your parents came to the rescue on various holidays when I did not have the funds to travel home to North Carolina. In my heart, they were bigger than life.

As I extend my deepest sympathy, it's a comfort for you and Florence to know that the two of you have been great caregivers. In my heart, I know that Mrs. Holloway was aware that she was loved by her children and grandchildren, which was a source of peace and contentment for her. Even though her condition limited her verbal expression, in reality she knew that you and Florence were courageous and made the best decisions for her welfare.

Enclosed is a love token for you and Florence, to be used as you wish.

Love,
Mildred and Pat

Mildred

Otis

Dear Mildred,

Thank you for all the support you have provided to me at the time of Mamma's death. Florence and I sincerely appreciate your thoughtfulness in sending the check. Mamma's work with Bowen United Methodist Church was so important to her, we have decided to make a memorial contribution to the United Methodist Women for their philanthropic work.

Our circle has been wonderfully supportive with cards and money and visits. Lydia came by and helped Florence and me write thank-you notes. Marilyn wanted to come but I thought I would need her more at Bryant's wedding (ten days after Mamma's funeral).

Thanks for always being there with a supportive hand and kind words.

I am now trying to get beyond the sharp pains of grief and sadness. I pray daily for understanding. I am enclosing a letter I have written to my mother in heaven.

Love,
Otis

My dear Mother,

On July 24th you took your final journey home. You were always a great mother, showing love, caring, and thoughtfulness. Thank you for the many things you taught me about life and loving others. You, better than anyone else, understood sharing and giving. I know that you must be celebrating with the Lord and all of those who preceded you in death.

Good works were always your specialty. And you achieved most of the things you desired during your life. In fact, you continued to make positive accomplishments after you became ill. There were the two nursing homes in Birmingham that you integrated. Florence, the family, and I were so proud of you. Five years ago, your work was not finished; now it is.

My brain tells me this is a time to celebrate, but my heart is truly sad; I will miss the warmth of life that I felt in your presence. You will always have a place in my heart where I can feel your love.

And now I pray for peace and confidence in knowing that someday we will be reunited with each other and our Lord and King. Amen.

Love,
Otis

Otis

Lydia

60

Dear Marilyn,

I missed my father so much today when I found myself facing some critical decisions alone. He was always the unofficial legal and medical advisor for our family, and we turned to him for advice on most of our major decisions. No one would ever have believed that he never graduated from high school because he was so knowledgeable about so many things and so articulate in communicating that knowledge to others.

When he suffered a fatal heart attack in 1976, I thought that my world had come to an end. While I was forced to be "strong" and provide needed moral support for my mother in the days that followed, I struggled for strength in my waning faith during moments alone. I can vividly remember crying and screaming throughout the two-mile ride home from my mother's house each day when I found myself asking my daddy, as if he were there, "Why did you leave us? What are we going to do without you?" and "Lord, why did you take MY daddy—a man so important in so many people's lives—rather than one of the many people occupying space who wants to die?" Of course, the God I questioned was the same God that brought me through the devastating effects of Daddy's and J.T.'s deaths and still helps me maintain some degree of balance. Somewhere in the midst of those fits, or in my frequent visits to the cemetery for a while, I learned to rely on my own resources and to build upon my inner strength.

Love,
Lydia

Dear Otis,

When I experienced the biggest loss of my life—Mama Luke's death in 1978—I remember the letter and telephone call from you even though you were unable to be there in person. I am enclosing a copy of that special letter as it was written in 1978. It will always command a special place in my heart and it will always be handy as I place it in my special archive of memories.

Then, Otis, you were there last fall when I had the biggest shock of my life, the unexpected death of a childhood friend. Chad and I had shared many disappointments and many happy occasions. Each day I smile at reflections of our lifelong friendship. His loss has created a void in my life, but I will always cherish his memory.

Marilyn also offered comforting words during this very difficult time for me. These friendships have been very special for me. Your consoling words are a way of life and a great cushion for a grieving heart. Trust me when I say true friends are rare. I am very thankful to God that our paths crossed. May God bless you always.

Love,
Mildred

Mildred

My dear Mildred,

My heart is very heavy today, for your mother was a real and rare gem, and you know that I thought that she was a very special person in my life. I want very much to be with you at this time but will be unable to. Please use the enclosed check as you wish.

Mama Luke had a very rich legacy to leave the world—her children (especially you) and all of her grandchildren and great-grandchildren. You must find great consolation in knowing that you and the family provided the best possible medical care and a totally loving and caring family.

I will continue to say a prayer for you during the difficult moments that you will experience for a long time. You have the strength, I know, to endure the pain of losing your mother.

I will be in touch with you very soon—when you return to St. Louis.

Love,

Otis, Charles, and Bryant

Otis

Dear Marilyn,

There must be some truth to the saying that when a dominant flower is plucked from a garden, the surrounding ones begin to sprout and grow. Not only did I learn to develop more fully and rely more upon my own strengths, but I watched this development take place with others in my family.

When Daddy died, J.T. emerged as the dominant male in my extended family. Everybody (my aunts, uncles, mother, grandmother, and myself) leaned on him in much the same ways that we had all leaned on Daddy.

When J.T. died, the torch was passed to my uncle, who transcended his physical and mental problems and became a real source of dependability and strength for us, especially for my mother. He became much more useful than even he had ever dreamed he would become. Someone had to do it, so the Lord enabled Uncle John to be there for us. At the same time, I watched my son mature beyond the stage of mischief and move toward becoming the mature, responsible adult that he has since become. I can't help wondering how long it might have taken Uncle John or Judson to develop such strength and independence if Daddy and J.T. were still alive.

Love,
Lydia

Lydia

Dear Mildred,

In November I faced the grim reality of the shortness of life when my friend Stanli died in Cleveland at the "young" age of fifty. Stanli was on my staff at Job Corps in Charleston, West Virginia. Then she was young, energetic, and full of dreams about making things better for young people. She carried her dedication to the development and education of children to Cleveland. Stanli and her husband, Tom, were the parents of one birth child and four adopted children. I wrote to Tom to express my feelings about Stanli. I would like to share these expressions with you.

Stanli and I shared some wonderful memories of our days with Job Corps and our stay in Washington. Her life was so full of memorable moments, and I feel honored to have been a very small part of Stanli's saga. Now when I think of Stanli, I recall some of these memories and relish them all over as best I can. Added to events based in reality, I visualized Stanli at the beach, with a gentle breeze, in a boat on a tranquil sea, sailing out to some unknown destination with that wry "I've got a secret" Stanli kind of smile on her face. And then I feel a calm longing to know what she is up to now. Somehow I think that perhaps she is continuing to be our great manipulator, but in a very benevolent way. Yes, death is inevitable, and so is life. But the loss of a friend or mother is indeed painful.

Love,

Otis

My dear Mildred and Marilyn,

Thank you both for the card and article on grief and for your comforting words on the telephone. As you know, I have been feeling extremely sad because of the illness of our friend Jo in Milwaukee. Fred and Jo are two truly special folks in our lives. They seem more like family than friends. Charles and Fred have been friends since they were school chums. And the friendship has been continuous. Realizing that her health was not good, Jo retired from the Milwaukee Public Schools in February, after thirty-plus years. Early in January, Fred and Jo called to tell us that they would not be making the trip to Florida as promised because Jo was on oxygen and could not fly.

So Charles and I decided to go to Milwaukee for the Memorial Day weekend and to take them Jacksonville in a bag. We collected shells, a sand bucket, Jacksonville posters, T-shirts, key chains, etc. In addition we packed a cooler with shrimp and we prepared shrimp Creole and fried shrimp. For the "kids" we took coloring books. Together we viewed a photo album and video of Bryant and Maria's wedding. We then watched the video of Jo's retirement program and reception. What a wonderful opportunity to experience just how special Jo is to so many people.

One evening the kids rented the movie <u>Forrest Gump</u> for us to watch on the VCR. Throughout our visit, Jo was in a great deal of pain. Surprisingly, she mustered the energy to accompany us on our search for authentic Wisconsin cheeses and sausages. I admired her total involvement in the usual day-to-day

Otis

concerns of the household. We are thankful for the time we had with Jo and Fred and the entire family during this visit.

Recognizing that Jo will not recover from the cancer that is destroying her body is both difficult and extremely painful for me to accept. Jo is an extraordinary woman who managed home, family, career, community service, church work, and life with the greatest of ease. Through the years Fred and Jo's home was home to us whenever we visited Milwaukee. We mortals are never ever prepared for death, but age fifty-six seems far too young for Jo to die. Mildred, I know exactly how you felt when your friend Reuben died a few years ago.

I am a Christian with an understanding that life on this earth is transitory. Spiritually, I even know that in death we move on to a better place of peace and happiness. Yet there is a feeling of loneliness when I, knowingly, am faced with the death of a loved one. Jo remarked that she did not know what was more difficult, knowing that death was imminent or dying suddenly as in an accident. She said, "I think it is harder for the family and your loved ones to know that you are facing death." I said, "This is one of those things in life that we have no control over."

She went on to talk about how a minister had given her Scriptures to study and that she had found great comfort in reading the Bible. The thing that was not said, but that I felt sure of, was the fact that she was preparing herself and trying to prepare her loved

Otis

66

ones as well. However, I worry, as surely she must, for the well-being of Fred (her husband of thirty-three years) and the kids (aged twenty-seven, twenty-nine, and thirty-something). Fortunately, they are all in Milwaukee and available to help out as best they can under the circumstances.

Until about a week or so ago, Jo was actively involved in the decision making regarding her last days and the treatment she would or would not take. I don't know exactly what her diagnosis is, but it is a form of lung cancer for which there is no known treatment. She elected not to do those things that "might," but probably would not, be helpful. She also elected to remain at home with the help of hospice nurses and surrounded by the family. Six years ago she was diagnosed with leukemia. With treatment, the disease went into remission and the quality of her life was very good. She continued to work, enjoyed cruising, traveling, and her usual activities. Since the beginning of the year when the present cancer was diagnosed, she has been in constant pain. This form of cancer is extremely aggressive.

To cope with my feelings of pain and helplessness in this situation, I find that I must talk about exactly what is happening with my friend and also with me. And so, thank you both for listening and reading. To cope, Charles and I remain in touch with Fred and the kids by phone. We want them to know that we love and care about them all and show them in some small way that we are walking along with them on this terribly painful journey.

Otis

Finally, I read my Bible, recite the 23rd Psalm, and say special prayers like the following:

> Merciful God, in your boundless compassion, console us and give us faith, amidst things we cannot understand, to see in death the gate of eternal life. (Book of Common Prayer.)

The past few months have been filled with death and grief (the disappearance of one of our student leaders at the university and the discovery of his body five months later, and the deaths of two of my cousins within one week). So I have had to focus over and over again on experiencing pain and then trying to move beyond the emotional to the spiritual level of understanding. Again, thank you both.

Love,
Otis

P.S. June 26, 5:40 A.M., CST, Jo Lawrence died.

Dear Marilyn,

In addition to the devastating losses that I have experienced through death, I have suffered many other losses, such as the slim body that my husband admired in my younger days, most of my natural teeth, the bold, adventurous nature of my youth, and the ability to bear children. While I can't truthfully say that the weight that I have gained is a positive effect of the loss of a slender figure, I do consider the enjoyment of sex without the threat of becoming a nervous wreck of a mother at my age a real plus. I've never wanted to be younger, but I do wish I could regain my once healthy gums and sound teeth and the ability to dive from the high diving board. No matter how hard I try, I simply have not been able to go headfirst into the water for at least twenty years. I suppose I should consider the cautiousness that I have developed to be an asset in my "older" age.

All in all, through these losses, I have gained a newfound independence and self-reliance, an appreciation for "being with myself" or enjoying my own company, a respect for the different stages of life and the accompanying joys of each one, as well as an awareness of my mortality. The recognition of these "gains" has certainly helped to sustain me over the years. Now, I have an even greater support system in place to buttress me against losses in the future.

Love,
Lydia

Lydia

Marilyn

Dear Lydia,

It took me over a year to get things together to leave Iowa for California. And it took even longer after I realized my life there was killing me before I decided to leave. It is really true that when one is ready to make a change, the opportunity will come. It was only because I was so desperately unhappy that I managed to face the fear and confusion and uncertainty and move toward change. I had one friend who believed in me, who restored a bit of the old faith I had in myself. I'm sure that without his confidence in me, I'd never have managed.

After the confusion and torment of being between the old and the new, one would think a new beginning would be welcomed. Hardly! Every doubt and fear I had experienced returned to haunt my tremulous steps. I tell you, it is easier, much easier, to go back and try keeping the old ways together than to fight the fears and move on.

Fortunately, a major change requires a lot of action. Finding a place to live, establishing oneself in a new position, and making new friends all demand time and attention. I just had to keep putting one foot in front of the other and keep focused on how much happier I was. Only three weeks after being in San Francisco, I knew I would not go back to Iowa even if I ended up waiting on tables for a living. Happily, it never came to that. Starting new parts of my life now is not any easier, but I can take comfort in having survived the big beginning back then. Also, I have so much more support now. I have my wonderful friends and my wonderful grown-up boys.

Take care, much love, *Marilyn*

Dear Lydia,

In the middle of confusion it is hard to consider endings. It's sometimes even hard to recognize that honorable closure is needed. As we are trying to find a path through our major transitions, many relationships, ways of dealing with daily activities, even parts of our younger selves, must be relinquished. Change seems to have three primary parts: ending the old, figuring out what to leave and what to bring forward, and getting on with the new. Insofar as we can clearly leave the old, the analysis and new direction become easier.

We each have our own style of ending. Some run away too soon, some cling on too long, but all suffer intense feelings that relate both to the current ending and to old endings from the past. I tend to take my time, try every option available, before admitting that the end is here. Especially when that end is the end of a romantic relationship, I need to allay guilt by making sure I have tried all I know to make it work. Only then can I make an honorable ending and leave feeling guiltless. My style has kept me mired in old relationships too long and now may be keeping me in my current career too long. But it is my style, and I have come to accept the fact that I must cry and mourn the old way before I can move on.

I think endings are so difficult for most of us because we must necessarily leave a part of ourselves behind—that part that was something special to someone, played some role on the job, and most likely was amply rewarded. Even if the rewards were meager or the role had become painful, at least I knew who I was expected to be and where I fit in

Marilyn

with the others. When I leave that part behind, I experience confusion and sadness and sometimes a fear that I will be nothing if not the old self. And so I prolong the ending, saying tearful good-byes, making promises to keep in touch, mourning the loss of that particular reality. Only then do I know it is truly over. Some people do not realize that an ending needs attention. They brashly forge ahead into a new space before attending to the end. Unfinished business will always show up again, blocking the way until the process is completed.

My childhood friend Diane spent years not ending her old marriage. No new male companion ever measured up to the man she left. The new life she built for herself never measured up to the one she had left. She could analyze the old love's shortcomings and tell why it didn't and couldn't work and still let herself be at his beck and call. The old life, old expectations, overshadowed her for ages. All the workshops, books, and therapy she tried were ineffective until she let go of the old marriage and lifestyle. It required a change of heart and soul.

I truly appreciate your listening to all this stuff. Take care.

Marilyn

72

Much love,
Marilyn

Dear Marilyn,

Every ending should be accompanied by a new beginning, and I suppose, for me, that has rung true in most instances. Some of the most vivid endings that I can recall are the end to my marriage and child-rearing stage, and my son's marriage. These are probably most prominent in my mind because I suffered a new aloneness that I had never experienced (and hope I will never experience again). When my husband died just after our son had gone away to college, I was faced with being a single parent as well as being a single woman. Either would have been devastating enough alone. J.T. and I had spent a lot of time planning how we would spend our newfound freedom, traveling and visiting long-lost friends. Unfortunately, these plans never materialized for the two of us because J.T. passed before Judson had been away from home two months.

The next four years were a real struggle for me because I wasn't well prepared to face parenthood alone. As a result, I made a lot of mistakes. With my son, I overcompensated for the loss of his father by showering him with more than he needed. I was determined that he would not suffer for anything that I could provide for him. After all, it wasn't his fault that he now had only one parent. What I ended up doing was giving him too much of some things and not enough of the really important things (like quality time) that he needed. I knew that his childhood had ended, but I subconsciously tried to encourage his continued dependence on me. Maybe I was afraid that he would not need me again, or maybe I didn't want to be alone, but eventually, we both adjusted to

Lydia

the indisputable fact that he had to grow up and would have to assume responsibility for his own life. Thank God he grew to be a responsible adult in spite of my blunders.

When he became engaged to be married, I convinced myself that I would not lose a son but gain a daughter, so I thought I was adjusting to another "ending" quite well—until the day after the wedding. All of a sudden, a gloom came over me that those who were around me every day noticed right away. I thought I was happy over the marriage, but I must have been depressed that another phase of my life had ended. Well, after all, her family was large (three sisters and a brother, a mother <u>and</u> a father, a large number of aunts, uncles, and cousins on both her mother's and daddy's sides), while mine had dwindled to me, my mother and uncle in town, and a sister and two brothers out of town. Now just where do you think he and his wife would spend vacations at home? In my quiet home or in the home where the crowds tend to gather? Quite possibly my fear of losing him to her family had something to do with my depression the week after the wedding. Otherwise I thought I was perfectly happy with everything! Another ending had occurred and it was my responsibility to usher in a new beginning.

Most other experiences for me seemed more like natural transitions from one stage to another, rather than an ending and a new beginning. Now I'm having to face another ending, the end of my youth, but that deserves special attention in another letter.

Love,
Lydia

Lydia

74

Dear Lydia,

My most painful experience during change has been those periods when I felt disoriented. What existed didn't feel right, there seemed to be no choices available, and a future dream was the furthest thing from my mind. I felt truly lost. I needed to stop struggling and experience emptiness, not escape it. Between the death of an old life and birth of a new one, there is an empty crossing.

The hardest lesson for me, but one that kept me from messing up one more time, was not to act for the sake of acting. To be still, be quiet, and wait for clarity was pure torture. I wanted to do something, even if it turned out to be less than optimal. Taking time, figuring out why I was so uncomfortable, keeping on with the taxing, boring routine, were really lifesaving tactics. Your best advice was telling me to take care of myself in little ways and to take time to be alone. It takes practice to learn self-care and to realize that in solitude, awareness thrives. I still sit and meditate in the morning and walk by the ocean at least once a week. I keep chocolates in the fridge and prepare food for myself with the same care and thought I formerly reserved for planning dinner parties.

I will also be eternally grateful to you for being such a good listener. It is so important to have someone to talk to. My thoughts and feelings get sorted out in a clearer way when I try to make you understand. And you always seem to understand.

Much love,
Marilyn

Marilyn

Dear Lydia,

Just yesterday I was reading Angie's book (she's the teacher I've been working with for the past year). She quotes a book that lists six categories of loss: of attachments, turf, structure, a future, meaning, and control. I think my severe anxiety around career issues in 1989 probably stemmed from a feeling of loss of control. I felt used and misused and unable to envision a way to make things better. Our discussions have certainly restored my hope for a happier career situation, and our meetings illustrate how that takes place. My actual job is also better, which seems to be a by-product of the positive energy we generate together.

Love,

Marilyn

Marilyn

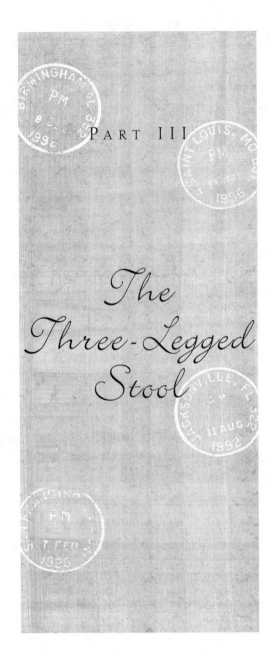

PART III

*The
Three-Legged
Stool*

Marilyn

Dear Lydia,

I am back on our favorite subject of relationships. We are always talking about our men, our children, our sisters and brothers. It is a preoccupation that feels natural. Our personal updates are essential and serve as the starting place whenever a group of women friends meet. As we grow older, we realize the importance of nurturing relationships, not only for ourselves but for all women during their middle years.

Meaningful interaction between two or more persons requires a structure in which the relationship takes place, the expenditure of energy by all involved, an intention for the relationship to continue or dissolve, and personal risk when the decision to be involved is made.

As we transit the middle years, from our relationship to self, let us consider what is of value to the soul, what has served well but is past its prime, and what we need to carry forward. For another person, it is important that we foster soul growth and note if we are aiding or standing in the way. We must consider what that person needs and accept the answer, even if the answer is "Nothing." The mood and temper of any gathering is important to note during group interactions. Our roles may change from leader to follower, from fostering a majority view to being part of the loyal opposition. In any case, our circle will work best when we are true to ourselves.

Love,
Marilyn

Dear Mildred,

As you know, I have not been a person who can hang on to misery and sadness for long periods of time. I feel thankful that the hard times of life have been limited. Several years ago I adopted a practice of thinking ahead and working out problems long before they occur. Once the inevitable does happen, then I seem to be more prepared and able to cope with the situation.

For example, when Bryant left home to go to college, I shed no tears because I had already done so the summer he was fourteen. That summer I experienced an overwhelming feeling of impending loss. The feeling was so painful that I cried whenever I thought about the fact that Bryant would be leaving home in four short years.

I kept thinking of all the things that I wanted to teach him. I systematically embarked on providing him with various crash courses. I taught him how to do the laundry, giving him full responsibility for washing, drying, and folding his clothes weekly. Then there were other crash lessons. When he finally left home, I was ready and so was he. There were no sad moments, no lonely feelings.

Your ability to be positive in the face of adversity has always been an inspiration to me and that is why I find a conversation with you so helpful. You have a real gift to be an advisor to others. May God continue to bless you, my friend.

Love,
Otis

Otis

Marilyn

Dear Lydia,

Last week Susan, a woman in my Sebastopol circle, told us about her adult daughter coming back to live with her and expecting a child in three months. I think it's great that she'll have a grandbaby right there in her home.

I was reminded of an old fantasy I have had to release. I had a picture in my head of myself and my husband living in the same neighborhood as my boys. I imagined big family gatherings about every six months. I imagined the boys stopping by for coffee, grandchildren coming in for cookies and chocolates. I planned to take each grandchild shopping for school clothes in September. November and December would be filled with Christmas preparations, helping each grandchild find presents for their parents and friends, teaching them how to make Christmas cookies and wrap beautiful gifts. I would take them swimming or fishing in the summer and attend all their football, basketball, and baseball games, or track meets, or whatever. I wanted to spend time with each son, daughter-in-law, and grandchild one-on-one, so I could listen carefully to each and get to know and appreciate each one.

In fact the boys are not too distant, but far enough to preclude a spontaneous "Let's have lunch" when a spare moment comes up. The comfort and joy of a big, extended family close by is not likely to happen. I am grateful that I see the boys often; they are very good about keeping in touch.

Take care, love,
Marilyn

Dear Otis,

While traveling to visit James III and his family in Minnesota recently, I met a woman at a rest stop who reminded me so much of Big Lil, a woman in North Carolina who had a big influence in my life. I met Big Lil after my freshman year in college, when I worked my first summer job in the tobacco factory. I shall never forget the day she said to me, "Young un, you don't plan to stay here to work forever, do you? You in college, right?" I said, "Yes, ma'am." "Well, if you're a good worker, the foreman is going to offer you a regular job, but don't you take it," she said. "I don't want no young Negro woman ending up wearing a bandanna for life. They don't treat the workers right and you won't have a chance to make anything important of yourself. Now, I don't want no back talk, gal. Just don't take no steady job here." I was a struggling student and the money looked good, but I gave serious thought to what Big Lil said.

One day near the end of my summer experience, the white foreman appeared on the scene and told me that he needed to talk to me during my five-minute break. Big Lil winked her eye at me. As I was leaving for my break, she whispered to me, "Gal, don't be no fool, remember what I said." When I talked to the foreman, I could feel Big Lil's presence in that room and I felt she was sincerely interested in my welfare. As the foreman continued to point out all of the pluses of my job, I could hear a voice saying, "Gal, don't be no fool." Then I made the first big decision of my life. I rejected his offer. When I went back to the assembly line, Big Lil winked at me and said, "You did the right thing."

Mildred

81

I have come to appreciate more and more folks like Big Lil, my mother, and my father who truly appreciated—and valued—education. While they did not have an opportunity to go very far in school, they recognized its importance and transferred their motivation to the younger generation.

Love,
Mildred

Mildred

Dear Lydia,

My experiences with mentoring were with a white male. There were no alternate choices in academic anesthesia. The association was difficult because it was tainted with barely suppressed sexuality. It's fair to say that my career advancement would have been extremely difficult, if not impossible, without his assistance. I learned research techniques, scientific writing, and had access to all the support of his established laboratory. He assigned small projects to me and oversaw their completion and publication. He arranged access to funds required to do the experimental work. He also invited me to picnic lunches in the park, or on the beach, or just in his office.

We went to the ballet and dinner a few times over the years, actually only once without others along. Nothing improper happened on any of those occasions. Still, I was uncomfortable and unhappy with the arrangement because it was clear that it existed entirely at his discretion. I felt that I must smile and please and play the role of ingenue to director. He had total control and could withdraw support at any time. Merit would be of no consequence. Over the years I moved away from research to a combination of administrative activities and finally, happily, to clinical anesthesia. Unfortunately, there are still too few mentors available for African Americans or women in academic medicine. Hope the picture is better in education.

Much love,
Marilyn

Marilyn

83

Marilyn

Dear Lydia,

For the first time in my life I have the possibility of forming a healthy mentor-student relationship. At present I am one of many students Angeles Arrien has in her classes. Her sincerity and concern allow me to feel that she would be available should I need her. I plan to study with her indefinitely and expect that the contact could become more personal over time. She certainly exemplifies the direction I wish and plan to follow in my life.

Historically the mentor-student relationship was father-son or mother-daughter. Later the apprenticeship became a primary way of training for a trade or profession. Out of that grew the tradition of older, successful persons leading their younger colleagues toward prominence. In most cases the mentor chose someone in his/her own likeness, especially gender and race. It is a continuation of the old "keep it in the family/clan/tribe" pattern of human behavior. It places women in general, and women of color in particular, in the position of having to create success with little in the way of support and guidance. I feel lucky to have as my dear friends three black women who have achieved professional and personal success. Take care.

Much love,
Marilyn

Dear Otis,

Today is my deceased mother's birthday, which I will celebrate in my heart. I will also deliver a bouquet of flowers to her grave. I always become teary on this day even though if my mother lived, she would say, "Do not mourn the dead, just keep the legacy alive and the love in your heart."

Mama Luke, as she was affectionately called, was my rock. Even though her formal education was limited, she could outshine anyone I know in common-sense and wisdom. She knew when to give advice and she was a good listener, too. She was a master of perception with unusual wit and foresight.

I will never forget the day after my high-school graduation when Mama Luke chose Talladega College for me. A high-school teacher had talked to me about Talladega, but because of my family's limited budget, I informed her that I did not have the financial resources to attend college away from home. I thought I should work and attend a college near home. Mama listened and said, "If you supply the brains, then I will get an extra job and supply the finances for you to go to Talladega, if that is your wish." This she did, and I will never forget the sacrifice she made for me.

Often I thanked Mama Luke for allowing me to attend Talladega College, for it was there that I increased my circle of lifetime friends. Meeting you, Otis, and Dr. James O. Hopson made college both rewarding and meaningful from the beginning.

Send up a prayer for me, friend.

Love,
Mildred

Mildred

Lydia

Dear Marilyn,

During the summer of 1958, following my graduation from college, I worked as a counselor at a Girl Scout camp and was "adopted" as a mentor by a talented 10th-grader who sought my advice regularly. Through her remaining years in high school, her short stint in college, and her two marriages, we have maintained a closeness that has been more characteristic of sisters than mere friends.

Our relationship was muddied in the early years by an unfortunate experience that I had with her mother over what I thought at the time was a well-meaning gesture. I knew that she and her mom had a communication problem because she told me how difficult it was for them to talk. When her mother approached me to get advice on their relationship, I thought she was sincere, so I shared with her some pretty personal things that her daughter had told me. I thought it would give her some much needed insight into their relationship. Much to my surprise and disappointment, she confronted her daughter with the shocking news—"You're always putting your friend Lydia on such a high pedestal, but let me tell you what your good friend told me"—and proceeded to tell her all that I had said, as if I had deliberately violated a trust. I was afraid her mother would jeopardize our friendship permanently, but my friend knew that what I had done was not done with any maliciousness but with every intention of helping her. Because of her confidence in me, our relationship has endured and we continue to provide inspiration for each other.

Love,
Lydia

Dear Lydia,

You won't believe what a disaster my trip to Europe turned out to be. The countryside was beautiful and just experiencing the different cultural overlays was interesting and fun, but my friend from Minnesota turned out to be a real jerk!

The first sign (as in portent) that the trip might not be wonderful was when our anticipated upgrades to first class didn't come through. He made a big deal about using United Airlines so he could get his miles and use his points, so when that didn't work he was upset. We ended up in the middle two of a five-per row in "steerage." Actually, that's where I always ride so I just disappeared into my book until it was over.

The second sign was when he and I went to a dinner with colleagues and he verbally attacked me about some educational practices entrenched at the university. It was embarrassing and inappropriate, and to this day I have no idea what provoked the discussion or why he felt I was responsible for all the ills he apparently suffered during his stint there.

After that night, he became increasingly difficult. A couple of times when we were out walking, he'd try to walk too fast, presuming I couldn't keep up or would ask him to slow down—fat chance!! I focused on being gracious and considerate, speaking only about the weather, the food, and the treasures we saw. I think if he'd relaxed, I would have been happy to attempt a reconciliation. However, it seemed neither of us knew how to break the icy barriers. He became upset about money, which I now realize was really an upset over power and control. We had

Marilyn

agreed to share expenses, but he was suspicious of my record keeping.

We left a few days early and didn't speak another word to each other after arriving at the Rome airport. I'm sure we'll never speak again. At least the experience was a lesson about how not to conduct a new relationship. Boy, can I pick 'em!

Much love,
Marilyn

Marilyn

Dear Marilyn,

Why is it so hard to believe that male-female relationships can exist without sex or romance? I never cease to be amazed at the number of women (and men) who look at you in such disbelief if you admit to having a close friend of the opposite sex who is not a partner in bed or pursuing you for that reason. I have had a number of men friends in my life who have been wonderful friends—even occasional escorts to public events—but who have not demanded sexual favors by the end of the evening.

If it were not for a few of these friends, I would not have fared so well in some of the other relationships that I've had. One who comes to mind immediately is my friend Milton, who counseled me through the "failed" relationship that I had a few years ago with the widower that dominated my every thought for entirely too long. Milton's wonderful way of allowing me to talk about it frequently over lunch kept me on the side of sanity and helped me to cope with it successfully. When I spilled my guts to Milton, he gently and cautiously guided me through an analysis of myself and the relationship and truly helped me to see the wisdom (or lack thereof) of my ways.

It felt good to share such intimate feelings with someone who understood the male ego and female psyche and who cared enough about me to tolerate the shoulder-leaning. If I had a dollar for each time he must have stifled himself to avoid making (or voicing) judgments about me or my love interest, I could probably afford a new car. I recall the relief that I saw in his face when I finally told him (a few years later)

Lydia

that I had put that relationship out of my mind and was going on with my life.

Milton and his wife are two of my dearest friends to this day, and I truly believe that it would make them genuinely happy if I would find someone who could love me for me and who would not allow me to stay on the "giving" end. They both knew that I wasn't getting half as much out of that relationship as I was trying to give. Let's face it: everybody needs stroking sometime, and believe me, after being alone since 1980, I can use a generous share myself.

I appreciate having a friend like you to share these things with, but it was equally good to have a male friend like Milton to share with. The therapeutic value of our relationship could not have existed if our relationship had been based on, or had involved, sex or romance. Am I strange, or does that make sense to another single woman like yourself? Thanks for letting me share such musings with you.

Lydia

I love you.
Lydia

Dear Lydia,

You should be in my writing class. We come up with the darnedest things, unexpectedly. Claire asked us to write about something we wanted for Christmas and didn't get. Eliza said that I wanted a man!! Where she got that from I cannot figure out, but she said it twice. Since I couldn't think of anything else, I decided to see what I had to say about getting a man. I expect a CANDID response from you immediately.

My first reaction to the idea of a man in my life is wariness. I wonder, what will he expect from me? How will I have to rearrange my life? There is not enough time to do what I am currently attempting; how can I fit in anything else? I cannot expect anyone to meekly come along with all my preferred activities. I am frightened of being forced to make too many compromises. Sunday morning I woke at 7:30, decided to sleep awhile longer, awoke again at 9:30, decided to make a cup of tea and read in bed. It was fabulous. I can see out to the trees around the house, the sun was streaming in through the skylight. I was reading a superbly engrossing mystery which does not require energy or critical thinking. It was heaven!! I read until 12:30. How can I choose to have those kinds of mornings with someone else around? The glorious silence will be broken, at the very least. What if he likes to walk or go out for coffee and bagels on Sunday mornings? How will I avoid falling into the trap of "pleasing," of going along with what he wants, since most decisions are not critical. I'll be sure to think, "Save your fight for something important." Then I'll give in and give in until I feel myself

Marilyn

drowning and walk out to save my soul. May as well stay as I am.

Frequently I miss the wonderful conversations one has with a beloved companion, the knowing and being known that feels so wonderful. Pleasures shared are pleasures doubled. I ache for what I imagine could be a deepening and lengthening and spreading ribbon of intimacy; for the wonder of shared thoughts and feelings and the safety thus created.

The intensity of my longing for a man is matched only by the intensity of my pleasure in solitude. At times like this, I understand why some hide from feelings. Opposites can be too much to handle.

Take care of yourself, my dear friend.

Love,

Marilyn

Marilyn

Dear Otis,

It's that day that creeps up on me every year: Mother's Day. I could be sad, but I choose to be happy. It gives me an opportunity to celebrate some very important women who have made a positive impact on my life—Mama Luke (my mother), Veen (my sister), Big Lil, Mrs. Lucille, and Mrs. Hicks. These are the women whom I have nominated and inducted into <u>my created</u> "Ain't I a Woman Hall of Fame." My selection is based on their high performance and super strength, both of which run congruently with Sojourner Truth's high level of determination to be the best that they can be, in spite of all the odds.

This Mother's Day, when I visited Mrs. Lucille in a nursing home, in spite of her weakened condition, she thanked me for always sacrificing some of my time to visit her. She said, "You have always been there for me through my ups and downs. I wish to thank you for always remembering me. As you walk through the forest of life, never destroy or kick aside stray branches that may seem to be blocking your path; for one or two of them will make good walking sticks one day." Then she paused to catch her breath and she continued, "You are my walking stick that I carved over thirty-five years ago. You have been a faithful friend; always present when I needed you and always there to make my ailing days a little easier." I began to mention the many favors she had accorded my family and me. Being a caring and sharing lady, she served as a surrogate mother for me during my early days in St. Louis.

We talked continuously for several minutes as I gave her water and then she asked me to pray with

Mildred

her, which I did. I watched, listened, and realized that my body will become old one day if I continue living. Shortly after our conversation, Mrs. Lucille died. She left a powerful message: Everybody needs somebody.

As I write this letter, I am sure that our circle will be a gigantic walking stick for each other. Our relationships have endured time, different locations, diversified jobs, and religious affiliations. I hope and pray that God will continue to bless us with each other's friendship.

Happy Mother's Day, Otis.

Love,
Mildred

Mildred

Dear Marilyn,

Most people who think they know me would be surprised to hear me say that I have always had difficulty with relationships. While I tend to meet and greet people well, I don't do well in establishing close relationships with people that extend beyond the superficial "Hi, how're you doing?" stage. As a matter of fact, while I want to be liked, I don't feel a need for developing a lot of close friendships.

I think I may be harboring a fear instilled in me years ago when my father admonished me not to allow people to get too close to me. "The closer people get to you, the more they know about you," he said to me in my early teens, "and the more they know about, the more they can—and will—hurt you." So the words "Don't let people get too close to you" have been a constant echo in my ears for the past forty-plus years.

Renewing old relationships with you, Mildred, and Otis has added new meaning to my middle years. Being able to share my innermost thoughts with women who genuinely care about me brings a fresh meaning to friendship that is so important at such a pivotal point in life. If what Daddy said is really true, all of you have the potential to destroy me by betraying the trust I've placed in you. More important is the fact that you also have the potential for accompanying me through the doors of old age and giving me the support that will help me to enjoy the coming years much more, and in a different way, than I have enjoyed those that have passed.

Love,
Lydia

Lydia

95

Dear Otis,

I wondered about our potential togetherness, for I had never dreamed that a dreamer like me would venture into lasting relationships with females. In the past, I believed that I could get along only with male friends because I felt they were a little more dependable than women. I now realize I was at fault for having these feelings. I feel a need to dispel the myth. Can I now fit the mold of being sincerely interested in the physical and mental growth of other females? At my age, I need a lot of nurturing—more mental and emotional than physical. Who could give the life vitamins that I need?

During a difficult time in my life, when I was afraid to consider retirement, I threw out the life raft and to my amazement I did not have to sail too far out to sea. Help was only as far away as an arm's reach, our circle. It was right there in those long-lasting friendships that spanned the U.S. Yes, we live in different locations, but the emotional multivitamins can be consumed by all with a phone call or a visit. And so our circle was born—created and perpetuated by four women who are caring and sharing dreamers, movers and shakers, professionals and homemakers, wives, a widow, and a divorcée. All may not have sailed on the same sea of experience in the past, but we are now in the same boat.

Love,
Mildred

Mildred

WINTER 1993

Dear Marilyn,

Being a widow has its drawbacks; I imagine being divorced has its own as well. One of the most difficult tasks I've faced as a widow is that of developing a lasting relationship with a man. I've had great sex, good conversation, and exciting romance during these years alone, but they have all been quite temporal (and never all from the same man). I think I just don't know how to build a lasting relationship with a man. After all, I haven't had to court for some time now. Sometimes I think, "I had one good marriage; who am I to think I deserve another?" Other times I think, "Maybe my prince will come along when I least expect him." Maybe the rules of dating have changed and no one bothered to inform me. Whatever the case, I seem destined to survive my middle years without a mate.

Now the importance of significant others, such as my friendship with you, Mildred, and Otis, has reached an unprecedented height. Between planning for retirement and filling my spare moments with service of some sort, I am too busy to worry about not finding another husband. While it would be great to have a compatible mate to grow old with, it would be disastrous to wind up with the wrong one. With the growing threat of AIDS, I find increasing solace in being careful about forming new relationships at this point. I can't tell you how important it is to me to have the kind of relationship with you that will allow me to discuss this sensitive matter in this way. Thanks for your shoulders and ears.

Love,
Lydia

Lydia

97

Dear Lydia,

I have had several phone calls from our mutual friend Leroy this past week. First he was anxious to ascertain that I would be in town during his next business trip here so he would know whether or not to plan to stay over the weekend. I said yes, the weekend plans would be fine, we could go up to the country or something. I also restated my intention to deepen our friendship without becoming lovers. He said, "Okay," but called back this morning to cancel, saying he was uncomfortable and felt like he was being put in a box. I guess he meant constrained. I decided to write him in an attempt to explain what I obviously cannot get across on the phone. I want to share the letter with you since it clarifies a lot of what I talk about when we discuss men or the lack thereof. After you read it, let me know if you think I overreacted.

Love,
Marilyn

Marilyn

Dear Leroy,

You didn't ask me for advice or comment, but I figured that several phone calls and an on-again, off-again weekend plan entitled me to have my say. A friend said to me just last week her therapist once told her that a relationship was like a three-legged stool. It needs communication, companionship, and passion in order to stand straight. I couldn't agree more. I have been in relationships that wobbled on one short leg and ones that fell over when two legs were shorter than the third.

Communication is the really hard leg to develop. There are so many general differences, cultural patterns, and personal styles, it makes finding common ground difficult. Somehow each partner has to find a way to keep the other current about thoughts and feelings. Some people speak volumes, others can say as much with a smile and a wink, and others seem to communicate telepathically. Whatever the style, as long as two people continue to learn about each other, it is possible to forge a solid bond.

Companionship is the easy one. Golfing, hiking, tennis, cooking, movies, reading, TV—the possibilities are endless. Shared activities are essential to keep personal attachments strong and to create time for sharing. Each one will definitely have solo interests and those shared with other friends as well, both of which help keep this leg strong.

Passion is about powerful feelings and extravagant enthusiasm, only one of which is sexual. Two people can feel passionately about a project, a cause, raising children, continuing to grow and learn, or even a sport. A shared passion creates a special, pow-

Marilyn

erful bond whether the feeling is about each other or an outside activity. Sexual passion is the most pleasurable expression of these feelings, yet is too weak to sustain the passion "leg" alone.

It seems to me that any couple would do well to spend time together, to speak openly and honestly, and to find a shared passion to complement and enhance their sexuality. If this sounds like hard work, it is—but worth it, I think.

You say over and over that you don't want to be alone. I'm fairly certain that having a lover in your life or even in your house will not solve that. We are one with the universe and each other, including the obnoxious jerk down the street we'd rather not have around. The sure realization of that oneness dispels all sense of aloneness.

I am quite content alone. I can also say that I wish for a man in my life. However, I insist on building a stable three-legged stool upon which to rest my black bottom. Without such a stool, I will just keep on down the road the way I am.

I will always love you,

Marilyn

Marilyn

Dear Lydia,

Our friend Leroy came to San Francisco as planned last month. We spent one evening together, his birthday, which was quite lovely. We agreed that we each had a very good time. I took him to a trendy restaurant that I have wanted to try for some time. At first the evening appeared to be headed toward a real "bust." Our main course was served before the appetizer we'd ordered to share and so the appetizer had to be canceled. This spoiled, or at least altered, the "flow" of the evening as I had envisioned it. Fortunately, the food was very tasty and he was relaxed, enjoying himself. He did not seem to be bothered by my "take charge" persona which emerged when I had to deal with the waiter's error. After dinner, we went dancing. Naturally we both loved that. He's such a wonderful dancer. I've always felt most connected with him when we are dancing.

We talked long and openly. It became clear that he wants a lover and I want a friend. Surprisingly, we agreed to let it be. It was a liberating decision. Our relationship is too important, valuable, and rewarding for either of us to abandon. I am delighted that we didn't engage in a power struggle, insisting that someone come over to the other's point of view. How very, very ADULT of us!

All else is well. I can hardly wait for our St. Louis meeting. See you soon. Take care.

Love,
Marilyn

Marilyn

Otis

Dear Mildred,

Witnessing Bryant's marriage to Maria caused me to pause and reflect on my marriage to Charles. We have nurtured our relationship for twenty-six years. Over time we have grown into very mature human beings.

My heart is filled with joy and memories of Bryant saying "I do." I only hope that as a husband Bryant will be as sensitive, attentive, thoughtful, and loving as his dad.

The wedding also afforded us the opportunity to see friends and family from far and near. I was particularly pleased that Iris and Joe came. They were married at our house in Tuscaloosa, Alabama, in 1979.

As you may recall, Iris moved to Alabama with us from Richmond, Virginia, where she was Bryant's baby-sitter. Once we moved to Alabama, Iris lived with us for two years and attended college (Stillman and the University of Alabama). She is now teaching special education students in Talladega County. To say the least, I am very proud of Iris's achievements. She and Joe have a good marriage and a very nice home. Perhaps being a friend and mentor to Iris contributed in some small way to her success. She and Bryant have always had a special relationship and I value her contributions to his life.

I now hope that Bryant and Maria will help others as they travel on. I am bringing pictures of the wedding to Kernersville for you to see.

Love,

Otis

PART IV

Ending
Midlife
Mental Mess

Lydia

Dear Marilyn,

Isn't it amazing how freely we exercise choices in our youth, grow to become traditional in our views, live a lifetime of staying within the confines of what is considered acceptable or traditional behavior, and revert to the free, creative spirit of our youth as we approach old age? In my grandmother's waning years, she showed all of us how to break out of the mold of tradition and do things that would help you feel better about yourself. When my mother gave her a gray dress for Christmas one year, Big Mama commented, "I may be a grandmother, but I don't have to look like one." An important lesson that I learned from her response to the gray dress is that we need not be bound by the expectations of others in our dress or in our daily actions.

I've noticed more and more hints of purple in your wardrobe these days. Is that your way of saying that you have the right to study shamanism if you'd like and feel comfortable with the decision? One thing is certain: As we exercise our right to make choices that are clearly not viewed as the "acceptable" or "right" thing to do, we must be willing to assume responsibility for those decisions. It seems a shame that we must grow fairly old before we feel secure enough to be comfortable with our real choices rather than to settle for those that others expect us to make. If we persist in doing so, we may be able to change what others expect.

Love,
Lydia

Dear Otis,

It has always been difficult for me to personally celebrate my attributes. As a budding college student in 1954, I could always see the positive in other classmates and would merely denigrate my own talents. It was only when Dr. Hopson invited me to be his secretary that I realized I was an important person with many talents.

Even though my parents were struggling with my tuition, I wondered about an on-campus job, especially working with Dr. Hopson. I respected him to the highest, but had mixed feelings about whether I could meet his expectations as a secretary. I had taken typing in high school and knew the hunt-and-peck system pretty well, but I never expected to type for the godfather of perfection.

When I reported to work the first day, I found a note from Dr. Hopson saying, "Welcome to your new job. Take your time, concentrate, and avoid making too many mistakes. If you do, don't worry about it because you will do it over and over and over again until you get it right. I do not accept anything short of perfection, but I have never made a mistake in choosing my secretary all these years and this is no exception." He left the office after giving me stacks of papers to be typed. When he returned several hours later, he glanced at the wastebasket filled with pages of errors and said, "You have passed the biggest test of your life. You had sense enough to discard some trash and keep some. You will make it in this life because you refused to give up. I hereby declare you my secretary." I owe a spe-

Mildred

cial debt of gratitude to Dr. Hopson, my mentor, who always kept me on my toes and refused to allow me to give up or feel sorry for myself.

Love,
Mildred

Mildred

106

My dear Mildred,

I thoroughly enjoyed your recent letter about your relationship with "Hop," which was distinctly one of mutual admiration. Self-esteem, like a mustard seed, requires a hospitable environment in order to assure germination. As a child (a seed), I was nurtured in a supportive family and neighborhood where folks actually believed I would be successful in all of my endeavors. Paradoxically, in this same community little girls were admonished to be nice. And of course nice girls didn't do a lot of things in those days. One of the things nice girls didn't do was brag.

Fortunately, my father taught me the importance of appreciating one's accomplishments. One of his famous pearls of wisdom was, "It's a mighty poor dog that won't wag his own tail." These words gave me permission to appreciate and enjoy my own achievements.

I have always had a gift for verbal expression. My mother said that she could not remember me ever not talking. I appreciate this gift whether it is exercised simply in a conversation or while giving a major speech before an auspicious body of scholars. In my current job, my boss, Roland Buck, recognizes this skill by requesting that I speak for him at various occasions.

Most of all, I appreciate my capacity to develop relationships. While I have been slow to establish new relationships in recent years, I have worked assiduously to bring established relationships to great depth. Our circle has provided me this opportunity.

Love,

Otis

Otis

Dear Otis,

I received your letters and they were heartwarming and interesting. I have always admired your multitalents. I always reflect on your speaking engagement at Shiloh Baptist Church, Winston-Salem, North Carolina. I was so proud to show you off as my friend. That was over thirty years ago and the memory remains. Do you remember? Continue to strive for excellence.

Sincerely,

Mildred

Mildred

108

Dear Marilyn,

You are truly a stabilizing force in my life and I appreciate you for it. Maybe if I could be near you on a regular basis and in the invigorating environment of a place such as San Francisco, I could find constant reinforcement and not have to wait several months to feel renewed. You are so good about advising me on things, I need to hear in your sometimes subtle, sometimes not so subtle way that if I could be closer to you and join you in some of the healthful activities that we discuss, I would surely look and feel a lot better.

One of the problems I have at home is that I have no friends who share more than one or two interests with me. I have club sisters whose company I enjoy at meetings. I have a few (very few) coworkers whose company I enjoy on the job (at least when we are discussing work-related "stuff"). I have bridge-playing friends whose interest in bridge approaches mine on that evening each month that we play. But I don't have any close friends who are making serious strides in embracing the "healthy style," and it is hard for me to get motivated to "go it alone." I appreciate your friendship and your willingness to accept me and love me, in spite of my shortcomings, and continue to believe in my ability to overcome these weaknesses and feel really good about myself. Thanks for being there for me, even if you have to grit your teeth and count backward to keep me happy.

Love,
Lydia

Lydia

Dear Mildred,

That time of year when you get to be the oldest for a few days is over. Today is my birthday and finally we are even again. You will never guess what Charles gave me for my birthday. Not diamonds, not a trip to Hawaii, not a fur coat (who needs one in Florida?). This year he gave me a healthy dose of self-esteem.

While viewing, as usual, <u>Good Morning Jacksonville</u>, I looked up just as Steve Smith, the weatherman, was saying, "This morning we wish a very happy birthday to Ms. Otis Holloway Owens, and her husband says she is still a mighty fine twenty-nine." I was stunned speechless. I can't convey just how surprised I was to see a photograph of myself covering the entire TV screen. Charles was watching rather smugly, delighted with himself that he had really surprised me.

I have been on cloud nine all day. My UNF colleagues sent me notes; former students, neighbors, and friends phoned to wish me a happy birthday and to comment on seeing my photo on TV. I feel as though I have been bathed in a healthy wash of self-esteem.

This unexpected gesture by Charles to make my day special was delightful and very much appreciated. What a unique way for him to say "I love you." You know just how much I value the relationship Charles and I share. For over twenty-seven years we have spun a delightful relationship based on love, respect, partnership, companionship, freedom, sex, intimacy, caring, and friendship. Our marriage has had a healthy dose of each of these, with the amount of each changing from time to time. I believe that now we have more of a balance. Over time, we have both come to appreciate the various ways of expressing intimacy other than just by engaging in sexual intercourse.

I have come to expect his gifts of back rubs or a glass of orange juice while I take a bubble bath. He can count on me for a manicure or a pedicure. Together we hold each other close, especially after hectic days at work, and quietly say that everything is all right as long as we have each other. In a more bizarre way, I feel that we both experience a special closeness during those times when we disagree and challenge each other's ideas. Keeping the lines of communication open have helped us through both the good and bad times. For us, you and Pat and Charles and me, these times have resulted in long-term relationships of thirty-five and twenty-seven years of marriage.

Why?

Love,
Otis

Otis

111

Marilyn

Dear Lydia,

Some days the idea of appreciating myself is so hard it feels foreign. It's those days when the sun's not out, I've been working too many hours, and everyone in the world appears distant. In those low-energy times when I need to focus on the positive parts of my life, the skill of appreciating and celebrating fades and fails.

One evening some years back, my dear friend Russ said to me, "You're looking especially beautiful tonight." I answered, "Thank you, but I don't think of myself as beautiful." He said, "You are and you'd better start appreciating it, because at your age you won't have it much longer." I was startled into considering my physical appearance from a different point of view; that is, what's right instead of what's wrong. I started noting when someone was complimentary and remembering times in the past when I'd been considered especially striking.

In the past year, a significant number of my acquaintances and relatives have died. This caused me to focus on my feeling about death and engendered a new level of appreciation of life itself. My teacher instructs us to celebrate life in our morning meditation and rejoice at the dawn of each day. I am grateful for the good health and good fortune I enjoy.

I also deeply honor and appreciate my good friends. They provide inspiration, a safe haven, and the sure knowledge that I am not alone. I have much to appreciate when I sit still and remember.

Take care, much love,

Marilyn

My dear Mildred,

I have a wonderful collection of memories of our friendship. My recent attendance at the 35th Talladega College reunion aroused feelings of my appreciation for our friendship at Talladega. Even after graduation, we managed to nurture our friendship through the years by writing, calling, visiting, and praying for each other.

Together we have shared special January birth dates, celebrations of baptism for the boys, vacations, weddings, births, deaths of our parents, and graduations. Before and after our marriages, we visited each other's homes. I traveled to Winston-Salem, St. Louis, and Kernersville, and you traveled to Mt. Meigs, Washington, D.C., Middleton, Richmond, Tuscaloosa, and Jacksonville. I suppose you missed Albuquerque.

I appreciate the fact that you have always been there encouraging me to "Go for it, girl." I imagine that there were times when I was moving from city to city and job to job that you must have wondered, "Just how crazy is my friend Otis?"

Your personal qualities have made you a valued and valuable friend. I appreciate your genuine integrity and sincere steadfastness. Your honest and frank opinions are always offered freely and directly. You have served to guide and even redirect me from time to time. Happily, I celebrate and appreciate our friendship.

Love,
Otis

Otis

Lydia

Dear Marilyn,

When I lean toward despondency, I usually make a list of my attributes/strengths and use it to remind myself how blessed I am and how many reasons I have for overcoming even the slightest depression. One of my most dominant characteristics has always been my pleasing personality and my ability to get along with most people. I can easily get despondent, though, when I think of the difficulty I have getting along with my boss—the first serious experience I've had in relationships that I have not been able to over-come. My once effervescent personality reaching out to others has now become a more reserved one, wait-ing for others to reach out to me. Underneath it all is the innate ability to relate to and get along with most people—truly a strength to be acknowledged.

My sister wrote me a letter in 1988 that I have kept until this day because it was such a beautiful tribute and capsule of some perceived strengths from her vantage point. I am sharing a copy of that letter with you. I think you'll understand why I feel so blessed when I read it.

Love,
Lydia

Dear Lydia,

I cannot thank you enough for calling me tonight with your good news. I told you that I really needed to hear or see something upbeat and hopeful after the day I had. After sitting through two regional workshops and a business meeting, I heard more about projects that make a difference in your brief phone call. You have the gift—and a rare gift it is—to maintain a genuine interest in service while participating in organizations which spend an inordinate amount of effort in giving big awards for little things. That dedication, commitment, patience, and perseverance, combined with your exceptional ability to maintain warm and caring relationships with people, give you the ability to mobilize resources for good which may otherwise be dissipated or wasted.

You prevent the dissipation by keeping the focus on the goal rather than the personalities (while being ever aware of the uniquely individual personalities of the persons you are dealing with). And you prevent the waste by cutting through the bull and allowing people who lack the patience for it to contribute to activities under your leadership.

In short, the more I see other people, the more I like you. Part of your special charm is the fact that you see yourself as a fellow traveler with others, while at the same time you maintain your individual principles and character. You accept others as they are without condescension or adoration, and that, in turn, allows them to accept and love you. Because you are the way you are, the best of the people you meet respect and love you the most.

When I said to keep up the good work, I could

Gwen

have said to stay as sweet as you are or just keep being you, because another endearing characteristic is that you do all the things you do in a manner that appears effortless. It seems, watching you, that the natural state for people to live in is to have a demanding full-time job, and spend major portions of spare time devoted to the service of others. Your exceptional intelligence, wit, and organizational skills make that time productive and lacking in drudgery for those who work with you.

I am proud to know you, sister dear. The fact that you are my sister gives me inspiration and hope.

With ever-increasing love,
Gwen

Gwen

P.S. I loved writing this. Gee, I feel better.

Dear Lydia,

Only recently have I come to realize the key role acknowledgment plays in our lives. A welcoming tone of voice, a smile when seen, a word of congratulation; all so simple yet all so vital. The big role of our circle in my life has certainly been the acknowledgment I've received from my sisters.

My teacher Angeles Arrien talks about the four categories of acknowledgment and the great healing value contained in acknowledging skills, character, appearance, and the impact we make on others. Our skills are so often taken for granted. I remember you telling us about a male colleague paraphrasing your suggestions and having the credit go to him. They didn't even hear your voice! That is such a common experience of women in our society.

Last month a young physician came to me and said that I'd inspired her by something I said at a student meeting many years before. I can't tell you how important that was for me to hear! One simple acknowledgment added such joy to my day and such reassurance that all the old efforts were not wasted.

The flip side of acknowledgment is invisibility. We can all remember not being seen or having our work ignored. It is painful. I use the memory of these pains to remind myself not to inflict the same pain on those around me. I hope to establish a habit of acknowledging so ingrained that it becomes second nature to me. I am eternally grateful to you for your constancy and clarity when you speak.

Take care, much love,

Marilyn

Marilyn

Lydia

Dear Marilyn,

As I approach my 55th birthday, I am reminded again of the need to "gift" myself. Since I have been a widow, I have found it necessary to reward myself with special gifts because I no longer have a partner around who would remember to do it. This new-found habit of mine does not in any way devalue the ways that my mother, my son, and daughter-in-law "gift" me on special days. Nor does it in any way re-duce the importance of the beautiful wishes that you always remember to send on my birthday (and other days as well). One of the first gifts that I can remem-ber buying for myself was a 1984 Seville—my gift for my son's graduation from college. After all, I was the one who had sacrificed for his education—he had a ball! Certainly I deserved a gift in recognition of this milestone.

On a different scale, I have tried to remember to pet myself on a regular basis by hugging myself with the seat belt when I get into a car, by getting my nails done regularly while I rest from the hectic pace of everyday life, and by treating myself to what I enjoy most—traveling—as often as I can afford it. Each time I do something for myself, I tell myself "I love you" and feel so much better that I've done it.

Love,
Lydia

Dear Lydia,

Please express to your mom just how much it meant to me to visit with her on Sunday. As you know, Florence and Bertram also joined me in my journey to Bessemer. Driving back to Birmingham, each of us noted how uplifted we felt after spending some time with Mrs. Lewis. Our visit was more than enjoyable. It was both an educational and spiritual experience. We spent a delightful time discussing local politics, sharing information about mutual acquaintances, looking at Lewis family photos, and reminiscing about times past. As I listened, I learned so much about the current happenings in Jefferson County.

When we arrived, your mom welcomed us with open arms. She continues to be an exceptionally beautiful woman. And she was looking very good. Every strand of her glistening white hair was in place, her skin was radiantly smooth, and her hands and nails beautifully manicured and polished. Mrs. Lewis is a perfect picture of poise, dignity, pride, strength, intellect, kindness, affection, and love in every aspect of her being.

Though her mobility is physically limited, she certainly is not isolated in any way. I observed that her wheelchair serves as a command post which links her to countless state and local officials, politicians, organizations, family, and friends who seek her advice, opinions, or knowledge. I am sure there are times when she uses her mobile phone to offer unsolicited advice as well. She would be awesome on the Internet. Seriously, Mrs. Lewis is indeed a special treasure, a reservoir of knowledge and wisdom. And, she is

Otis

OUR dependable cheerleader. You are indeed fortunate to have your mom so near.

As we talked, I felt a special connection with my own mother. Through the Alabama Federated Women's Clubs, our mothers shared a common commitment to the youth of Alabama. Your mom told us that the role of the Federated Women's Clubs as founders of the Alabama Industrial School in Mt. Meigs was completely excluded from the State of Alabama's history of the school. What can we do to correct this misstatement of history? I am upset that the vision, work, money, and sacrifices of countless black women could be eradicated so easily by a stroke of the pen. Even the property where the school is now located was generously given by a black woman.

Just before we left, your mom produced a camera from its position on the "command post" and took our pictures. As we were leaving, she gave each of us a Scripture card to read and requested that Bertram offer a closing prayer. Reluctantly, with Dorothy's prompting and promise that "It won't hurt you," Mrs. Lewis agreed to come outside to take a photo with us. We drove back to Birmingham marveling over your mom. We were amazed that not once did your mom give us a litany of her aches and pains. We learned a tremendous lesson about living life to the fullest from Flora Lewis.

Love,
Otis

Otis

Dear Mildred,

The materials you sent on building a healthy self-esteem were especially helpful in planning for my staff workshop. I found an effective exercise which demonstrated how past teaching can limit one's behavior. I am not sure it would be as effective in your work because you are working with children who may not be as "fixed" in how they look at themselves. As we grow older, we become conditioned not to paint outside the lines—to do things the "proper" way. Thus, the creativity of our real self is lost.

When Bryant was about three years old and already focused on sports, he decided to organize his neighborhood playmates into a "baseball team." Being the ultimate arranger, he decided he needed an official shirt and proudly named the team "The Green Tigers." He never even considered the lack of reality centered in the name Green Tigers. He didn't even know or feel limited by the knowledge that tigers are never green. I have saved that shirt to remind me of his childhood spirit, where tigers are green when you choose them to be. I certainly hope that he can carry this childlike trait into his adulthood.

More important, I pray that in our senior years, neither you nor I will ever lose appreciation of the reality of green tigers, purple cows, and pink elephants.

Love,

Otis

Otis

Dear Mildred,

What a joyous time we had on the telephone last night, laughing, reminiscing, and fantasizing. Afterward I thought about all of the joys in my life, and I'd like to share some of them with you:

Joy is the baby Jesus.
Joy is loving.
Joy is Charles.
Joy is walking on the beach.
Joy is feeling the wind and sun against your
    face.
Joy is hearing, "You are pregnant."
Joy is seeing Bryant.
Joy is smelling the fresh Christmas wreath at
    my door, a gift from Marilyn.
Joy is talking to Florence.
Joy is seeing the cardinals and blue jays frolic
    in the blooming azaleas.
Joy is writing letters.
Joy is talking to Bryant and Maria on the
    telephone.
Joy is knowing the risen Lord!
Joy is hearing, "Mom, I have a job."
Joy is walking with Mary.
Joy is taking a bubble bath.
Joy is eating ice cream.
Joy is hearing, "We have a publisher interested
    in the book."
Joy is thinking.
Joy is hearing, "It is benign."
Joy is getting together with our circle.
Joy is listening to God.

Otis

Joy is driving through the back roads of
  Alabama.
Joy is singing.
Joy is hearing Ella sing.
Joy is being with friends.
Joy is listening to the chatter of squirrels.
Joy is coming home to a clean house.
Joy is fishing with Iris and Joe.
Joy is catching a fish.
Joy is pulling the recalcitrant hair out of my
  chin.
Joy is being home alone.
Joy is finding your glasses, keys, and purse all
  at the same time.
Joy is talking to Carolyn on the phone.
Joy is the feeling of relief after the itch.
Joy is giving to others.

I pray that you may find JOY in all that you do.

Love,
Otis

Otis

123

Dear Otis,

Pat and I are just returning from our trip to Hawaii in celebration of my birthday and our 35th wedding anniversary. The trip was wonderful and it afforded me time to think about our years together. Here are my thoughts:

Mildred

> Joy is my 35-year journey with a spouse who has the patience of Job, amid the confusion of my days.
>
> Joy is a spouse who quietly exhibits a sense of strength. Pat does not allow anything or anybody to disturb his peace of mind. His motto is, "Think only of the best and expect only the best." When I am irritable or displeased with Pat's laid-back persona, he always emerges wearing a countenance so cheerful that it almost drives me mad.
>
> Joy is realizing, after many sleepless nights, that Pat's strength is quietness. So it is I who need the remodeling.
>
> Joy is watching Pat assign himself several chores around the house, such as washing clothes. I often wondered why Pat wanted to wash the clothes. I soon found out when one day I surprised him in the basement and discovered the washing machine going full-speed and Pat sound asleep, even though he tried to make it appear that he was working hard. The machine did the working and Pat did the sleeping.
>
> Joy is reflecting on the ups and downs of a 35-year marriage. We experienced it all: joy and

happiness, some mistakes, trials and errors, some frustrations. Through it all our love for each other, strength of character, wisdom, and stick-to-itiveness enabled us to climb to the highest mountains in this 36-year relationship.

Joy is being married to a guy who is neither Mr. Right nor Mr. Wrong, but Mr. In-Between. A guy who has taught me to listen without judging.

Joy is reading the cache of love cards that Pat has given me on every holiday for 36 years.

Joy is knowing that because of Pat's caring nature, we have endured a year's courtship and 35 years of marriage.

Joy is using a special yardstick to measure my emotional growth as I have experienced the best of times and the worst of times. The best of times outnumber the worst of times.

Joy is watching Pat turn 62 years old, retired, looking goooood, exercising every morning, and taking his vitamins.

Joy is knowing that our 36-year relationship together is more than a marriage, it is a friendship.

Mildred

125

Love,

Mil

Dear Mildred,

I thoroughly enjoyed your recent letter which reflected the joy you continue to share with Pat after thirty-five years. Would you believe that I remember your wedding as if it occurred yesterday?

As you may recall, my getting to North Carolina was a creative adventure. At the time I was at Syracuse University in graduate school, and money, a scarce commodity, was the reason that I could not afford to be a member of your wedding party. I was thrilled when our friend Thora suggested that if I could get to New York City, I could travel as her companion. Though blind, Thora has never really needed anyone to assist her in traveling anywhere. In those days, a companion traveling with a blind person paid considerably less than full fare. Consequently, this arrangement made it financially possible for both Thora and me to attend your wedding. I rode a bus from Syracuse to New York City. Thora met me at the Port Authority and took me by subway to her place. Together we traveled by train to Winston-Salem. Actually it was Thora who assisted <u>me</u>. When we go to New York in April, seeing Thora is a must.

From the moment I met Pat I knew that he was a genuine jewel and wonderful human being. After thirty-five years living with you, I now know he is also a saint. Each of us is fortunate to enjoy a long-term relationship with a special guy. This is truly amazing.

Love,
Otis

Dear Lydia,

It has been so good for me to hear from you often this last week. I'm sorry you are faced with the problem of your mother's failing health. I pray that she will rally and cooperate with whatever you and Gwen feel is best.

This holiday season is full of extremes for me. I either have a big smile on my face or I'm on the verge of tears. Sadness seems so near the surface, a nameless kind of sad stuck to the joy so tightly I can't feel one without the other. We are so totally, completely, and forever alone in this universe. For this reason, one of my most treasured joys is the company of loved ones. I delight in phone calls, visits, evenings out with dear friends, with my boys, and with any family members who come my way. Those moments of feeling connected are pure joy.

Many other joyful things occur to me: blazing sunsets, driving through the Sierra, walking along a beach, sitting in the sun, opera evenings, eating popcorn while watching my son Hill on TV, getting a massage, listening to the blues, and most important, reading a good book. Maybe I confuse joy with pleasure. I count as joy anything that makes me smile or laugh out loud. When I was younger there were joys associated with career advancements, romantic conquests, and material acquisitions. I am happy to report that I have outgrown those. I miss that special joy I felt when the boys were babies. I must be ready for grandbabies. You are lucky, two grands and so nearby.

Much love,
Marilyn

Marilyn

127

PART V

Fit at Fifty

Marilyn

Dear Mildred,

Your questions about proper exercise were covered in an article I saw last week. The writers suggest that the quality of our later years will be greatly influenced by the habits we develop now. Exercise helps keep bones strong, conditions and improves heart and lung function, and enhances flexibility. How well we care for these functions now will determine how independently we can live in the future. There is also the "feel good" experience inherent in exercise. A good workout improves the mind and helps reduce feeling stressed. A walk outside provides visual stimulation and all the benefits of being in nature. We are moving toward regarding our bodies as temples and therefore treating ourselves with love, care, and concern.

Our attitudes about food may or may not lead toward healthy living habits. The common extremes, yo-yo eating, dieting, and overindulgence in "comfort" foods, are antithetical to health. A goal to maintain balance between food intake and exercise is the most desirable attitude. We are continuously made aware of current opinion about which foods or food additives are considered healthy or detrimental. Experts currently advise a diet containing moderate amounts of all food groups supplemented by vitamins C, D, E, and beta-carotene. I have started taking vitamins regularly and suggest you do also.

Love,
Marilyn

Dear Mildred,

I grew up at a time when girls played with dolls and tried hard not to get hot and sweaty; in an environment where there were no parks or swimming pools in the entire town; when exercise meant calisthenics (boring) or running (too exhausting); thinking physical activity meant doing housework, mopping, waxing, dusting, cooking, sweeping, etc., etc., etc.

Over a year ago when Health Services offered staff a physical fitness program that provided a personal trainer, I gave myself permission to become physically active in a '90s kind of way. This program provided the structure I needed to get going and I felt so good at the end of the program that I continued a modified routine of "working out" three days a week. Intellectually, I have long recognized the importance of exercise to feeling fit, but putting the "me" things first has always been a problem. Besides, I was never really good at doing the athletic stuff. But now, at least I have a fitness goal for myself:

> Walk three times a week on the beach.
> Walk for thirty minutes at lunch.
> Cut down on the fats in my diet.

Last summer I took a beginner's swimming course and participated in aqua aerobics twice a week. When the weather turned colder, I couldn't get motivated to continue this activity. Help!

Love,
Otis

Otis

Dear Lydia,

The myriad of physical appearance issues constitute a major segment of concern as women transit the
middle years. I now share your disdain for shopping.
My reflection in the dressing room mirror was upset-
ting. Have you noticed how our changing bodies and
ever-changing fashions greatly influence our comfort
level at this time? From our teen years on, we choose
a clothing style that expresses the level of our self-
esteem and reflects our self-image. We signal the
group to which we belong or aspire. We signal that
we will fit in with the corporate culture, will bring
style and grace into an organization, have been
trained in all aspects of manners, will know what to
do and how to do it. We choose garments appropriate for the occasion, weather, locale, and activity.
Some of us indulge in "retail therapy" and buy
clothes to soothe our troubled spirits, to provide mo-
mentary pleasure and instant gratification. We attempt to fill a void in our lives with yet another
smashing outfit. Some women use clothes to enhance
their desirability and some simply wish for beautiful
adornment. Some cling to the outdated clothes, accessories, and hairstyles that prevailed when they
were young and felt attractive. Our choices are limited by economic considerations. We learn to adjust
our wardrobes to our economic and workplace reali-
ties, often at great cost to spirit.

We make choices about living with our aging
bodies. An early decision is whether or not to color
our graying hair. Popular marketing strategies push
heavily toward hiding the gray as our culture contin-

ues to worship youth. The medical community offers many choices for altering the effects of aging: face-lifts, tummy tucks, breast augmentation or reduction, liposuction of this or that. For some African American women the threat of the exaggerated scarring of keloids severely limits surgical choices and for others the economic burden is too great. The question now is, what choices will we make?

Love,

Marilyn

Marilyn

133

Dear Marilyn,

Did I tell you that I am participating in a continence study here at the university? When I started to experience some "leakage" while sneezing, coughing, or simply waiting too long to empty my bladder, I assumed it was just one of the perils of getting older. After reading an ad about the continence study, I discovered that it is not only a common problem with women over forty but, better yet, one that can be helped with proper training. Maybe because I have always discussed sensitive and personal matters rather freely, I responded to the ad immediately and am now getting the training (in muscular control) that could help me to alleviate the problem.

On my last appointment at the clinic, I asked the nurses why there weren't more women participating in the study. They believe that many women will simply not admit that they have such a problem, and if they do, they do not choose to make the kind of admission that would be evident in their enrollment in a "continence" study. And to be seen entering a Geriatric Clinic for such a study would certainly not make it any easier. (I must admit the most difficult part for me was walking through the door labeled "Geriatric Clinic.")

I have always said that men could handle midlife crisis a lot better if they would simply admit that they experience such a crisis. If they did, maybe doctors could help them through that critical stage, like they have helped women through menopause. Now, I realize that we women are in denial when it comes to some of the issues that we face in the aging (mellowing) process. In private conversations with a number

Lydia

of women, I have heard comments about them having "accidents" when they laugh or cough, but few of them are coming for help in such wonderful programs as the one that I am participating in now. Another admission I have to make is that I am a sucker for programs that offer "free" medical exams and ways of preventing potential health problems. The primary attraction to this study for me was that it offered some valuable help that I needed, and offered it free of charge.

The Women's Health Initiative has faced similar problems in recruiting significant numbers of women, especially African American women. When I made an appointment to be screened for that program, I could not believe the statistics on the number of women who were participating. Both of these programs have used a variety of strategies to recruit more African American women, but their efforts have not yielded anywhere near the number that they had hoped to get. Do you think the Tuskegee study scared us away from medical studies?

I'll keep you posted on my progress.

Lydia

135

Love,
Lydia

P.S. Six weeks later. It really works!

Otis

Dear Marilyn,

Thanks for your encouragement when we spoke on the phone last week. Now that I am approaching the new year, I will affirm my earlier goals to walk, cut down on the dietary fats, and not gain any weight in 1994. In addition, I will add the weight room to my fitness routine once or twice a week. Further, I continue to cultivate the spiritual dimensions of my life through prayer and meditation. The quest for peace is satisfying though continual.

Adopting a fitness lifestyle can be done later in life. I don't expect to become addicted to the routine, but since I seem to feel better when I follow the routine, then I will be more motivated to keep it up.

I suppose I have always known that exercise is good for me, but then there were all of those reasons, really excuses, not to do it. I don't have time; I'm a klutz; it's too exhausting; and on and on. Finally, I have found a really simple exercise that is supposed to be as good for me as most other physical activities, and that is walking. I now enjoy walking on the beach, listening to the waves, watching the surf suds, the seagulls, the ships on the horizons, the shrimp boats, and other folks walking on the beach. I have even scheduled walks at noon for thirty minutes. My friend Mary and I walk around campus after eating lunch. This is a very therapeutic experience, clears my head, and allows me to focus on non-job-related thoughts. Fitness is definitely in my future.

Sincerely,

Otis

Dear Marilyn,

When I think about healthy living, I often think of the words of a former colleague of mine: "If knowledge changed behavior, there is no way I'd still be smoking. No one knows more about the harmful effects of smoking than I, yet I continue to smoke." As far as knowledge is concerned, I don't have to be a trained nutritionist to know what I shouldn't eat and I certainly don't need to be an exercise physiologist to know the value of exercise to a healthy mind and body. In spite of this knowledge, I maintain the most sedentary habits of anyone I know.

When I was walking every morning, I felt good about my exercise program. After a year or so of this practice, I heeded the devil's call as he convinced me that I needn't walk in the cold of winter nor sacrifice an hour of sleep in the morning when I needed to rest. I know I need exercise. I know I need to eat less fat <u>consistently</u> rather than a few times a week. I know that I'm not fooling myself when I drink black coffee with Sweet'n Low while I'm consuming dessert.

Maybe the task of writing about my habits will prove to be therapeutic. I suppose it's clear that the effects brought on by my mother's physical problems, my failure to find happiness in a stable romantic relationship, the severe stress under which I'm operating on my job, and the increasing loneliness that I feel on a day-to-day basis are <u>real</u>. If I ever needed a break, I need one now. I can only be helped by a weekend with my friends.

Love,
Lydia

Lydia

Marilyn

Dear Lydia,

Why is it that those things which feel most restorative are the most difficult to fit into my schedule? I love hiking, especially with a dear friend in Marin. One day last summer we hiked from a ranger station on Mount Tam down to Stinson Beach and back. The trail down led through lovely groves of massive redwoods. Quiet cavelike spaces seemed livable. I had a feeling of being protected and almost caressed by the trees. Later we sat on a big boulder facing west. We could see waves breaking against the rocky shoreline and a big fat fog bank hovering offshore. The effort of walking fast, then stopping in a beautiful spot, was exhilarating.

We had a delicious lunch in Stinson, poked around in a bookstore, then headed back. The trail back uphill was in the blazing sun. We went through fields of tall golden grass, then followed a mountain stream. We found a little pool formed by fallen branches and boulders. The cold water felt wonderful on our feet as we sat, sort of whispering to each other in order to disturb the quiet as little as possible. Vigorous activity, good food, a good friend, and the comfort of trees and streams truly restore my soul. Surely I will find time to spend more days this way.

I hope we can go back to Jacksonville soon. We didn't walk on the beach last time and I missed that bit of our work. Take care.

Love,
Marilyn

Dear Marilyn,

When I was growing up, my mother always selected my clothes. When I married, my husband selected my clothes, at least the ones that drew the greatest compliments. I have always hated shopping, and as prices rose, I developed a growing resentment toward the idea of paying so much for so little in return. Usually when I shop, I am looking for something as specific as a long-sleeved white blouse. Seldom do I splurge and simply buy clothes because they're stylish or look good on me. As a matter of fact, I seldom try on clothes, and that's considered a no-no in shopping.

As a result of my lifelong attitude toward clothes, my personal style is reflective of whatever I have in my closet that fits. I admire people like Mildred who can accessorize so well and who can find good-quality clothes for economical prices, but this is clearly not a strength of mine. With my schedule, I could truly benefit not only from having a buyer to select my clothes, but also a personal valet who would see that my clothes were always ready for me to wear at will . . . someone who could immediately suggest how my wardrobe might be maximized with colors and outfits blended. Most women who are as involved in organizations as I am are probably much more conscious of dress than I am. Maybe with retirement in the foreseeable future, I'll take the time to strengthen this weakness. Who do I think I'm fooling? I would have to <u>learn how</u> to do it before I could use my free time in doing it. For now, the song "Give Me the Simple Life" is my theme. Let me be comfortable and clean and I can concentrate on what I'm doing.

Love, *Lydia*

Lydia

Mildred

Dear Otis,

After battling the bulge for almost forty years and restricting my diet to control my weight, I have decided that I have let life pass me by. For forty years, I have counted every calorie because I had a certain figure I wanted to maintain, certain clothes I wanted to wear, and an image I wanted to portray (the thin woman syndrome). Now, at fifty-seven, I wonder if it has all been worth it.

At a certain age one wonders what to do to prolong life. Sometimes we can classify this as running scared, especially when we read the obituary page and notice that many of the names we see listed are younger than we are and some were health nuts who carefully watched their food intake. A very close friend of mine, Chad, was a picture of health and reminded everybody to lose ten pounds. He always read food labels and evaluated ingredients. He exercised regularly, walked five miles a day, and kept his weight ten pounds below his desired weight. He prided himself on controlling his cholesterol and blood pressure through diet. Only two days after Chad and I last talked, a friend informed me that Chad had died suddenly from a massive stroke.

Healthy living is a puzzle to me. Is there any way to avoid real complications as we grow older and develop old-age symptoms, or do we just prolong the agony? This is not an invitation to a "pity party." Just looking for a few answers.

Love,
Mildred

Dear Mildred,

There are so many uncertainties in this life, but if we hang on to our faith in God, we can be assured that while life on earth may not be all peaches and cream, our eternal life with Him will be. Our conversation at breakfast this morning reminded me that we can only do our best to make this life a comfortable one. The Lord determines how long it will be—not our exercise regimen or our diet. It's all about feeling good about yourself while you're here, not about extending life. The matter of life is clearly not our choice to make.

So what can be accomplished by the supreme sacrifices necessary for healthy living? The ability to walk up two or more flights of stairs and not suffer from exhaustion after the twelfth step . . . the ability to sit comfortably in the tourist cabin of an airplane without your hips preventing you from reaching the controls . . . the self-esteem to try on clothes in a dress store . . . the stamina to have sex for a sustained period of time without succumbing to a wild panting that will run your lover from the bed . . . the ability to touch your toes, tie your shoes, or pick up something from the floor without falling flat on your face. All of these are obvious reasons for trying hard to maintain a healthy lifestyle and manageable size. We never know if we're destined to become invalids, so keeping trim and fit will make it a lot easier to be carried upstairs and onto planes to join each other for meetings of our circle. It all seems worth it to me; it's just doing it that seems so difficult.

Love,

Lydia

Lydia

Marilyn

Dear Otis,

I have been surprised by the recent emphasis on starting physical fitness programs at any age. Those articles previously featured young, svelte, already very fit bodies. Now the models are as likely to be forty in <u>Lear's</u> and even approaching sixty in magazines like <u>Modern Maturity</u>. It's reassuring to know I can start over at any time since I'm prone to lapses in my own program. I must say that it took months and months to get accustomed to regular exercise but now I truly miss it when I'm too busy.

I recently read that for women forty-five and up, the one thing they can do to remain healthy and avoid premature death is keep physically fit. Women generally live to an old age. The level of physical fitness they have will have a profound effect on their enjoyment of life and ability to function independently. A lifetime practice of regular exercise is like saving up for the future.

I recently started running again. Although the experience is quite different alone, it is still satisfying and out in nature and a good workout. Starting a new fitness activity is easier with a friend or in a group, but I've discovered that there is pleasure to be found alone as well.

How are your nature walks coming along? You are lucky to live in the South and to get to see all the varieties of plants that flourish in different seasons. Are you up to five miles yet? That seems an ambitious goal but a worthy one.

Much love,

Marilyn

Dear Mildred,

I understand your concern about the ultimate benefit of maintaining a healthy lifestyle. I too have watched many people with very healthy eating habits and exercise regimens fall prey to serious illness or "early" death, while many with no regard for what they eat or drink survive serious illness or avoid it altogether. My father, who died of a massive coronary, had not had any indication of a physical problem of any sort throughout his life until a few months prior to his death, when he was told that he had an enlarged heart. As a matter of fact, he came away from his annual physical examination with a "clean bill of health." When my friend and sorority sister died a few months ago, she had been assured that she had no heart problem—just a virus that antibiotics were expected to help. Her trip to the doctor the Thursday before she died was prompted by a persistent pain in her chest. She had an arteriogram the next day, not because of a suspicion of heart problems but to clear the air of that possibility. After the arteriogram, she was scheduled for emergency bypass surgery and never lived to tell us about it. This was particularly frightening to me, because I have had every test for heart problems except the arteriogram and have been assured, as she was, that my occasional chest pains are not a result of any problem with my heart. The mere thought that I could be functioning on such a level now and could be told any minute that I need bypass surgery is unnerving.

Love,
Lydia

Lydia

143

Mildred

144

Dear Otis,

What a fun day! I just happened upon an exciting weekday that I didn't expect. I was walking through Neiman Marcus and, to my amazement, there was a clearance sign. I paused, stopped, and convinced myself to go look and see what was happening. Everything in the section was 75 percent off and I had a field day. I scouted the clearance racks and started thinking about color-coordinated styles which already graced my wardrobe.

I couldn't resist buying a gorgeous $199 navy brocade jacket for $30, even though the matching skirt was nowhere to be found. After shopping around for several hours for a matching skirt, something told me to go back to Neiman Marcus. To my amazement the matching skirt was staring me in the face. The saleslady informed me that the skirt had been returned as soon as I left the store. I said, "The Lord sent this to me." She said, "Huh?" "Nothing," I said, "you wouldn't understand." I completed a beautiful rich suit at the cost of $60 ($30 for the jacket and $30 for the skirt).

I couldn't get home fast enough. I matched this suit with my navy blue shoes, white silk blouse with a pearl necktie, and a dainty little antique blue purse. Two weeks later I was invited to a very fashionable event. I didn't know what I was going to wear, but I remembered the outfit I had pieced together. This is one of those occasions where "Retail Therapy" paid great dividends—smiles.

Love,
Mildred

---

* Retail Therapy has been the answer to many of my "down" moments. Shopping seems to take my mind off some of my problems.

Dear Lydia,

It seems clear to me that now is the time to consider my own specific style of dress. My highest priority is comfort. I refuse to wear restrictive clothes such as control-top panty hose, or walk around on three-inch heels.

As much as I would like to disregard outside opinion, the fact is, one's clothing sends a message. It therefore becomes necessary to make sure the message broadcast is the one I wish to send. Several years ago I started wearing East Indian outfits which were beautiful and comfortable. They were soft, loose, and easy to wear. I had silk, very dressy ones and cotton print, very casual ones. I slowly came to realize that their "too ethnic" look was attracting more attention than I wished for and also spoke subtly of a culture that was not my own. I stopped wearing them. Now I look for big tops, loosely flowing skirts, extra-large T-shirts, and simple straight-legged pants, trying to retain the comfort and freedom of the Indian clothes without the message.

At one time I had the idea I should dress in a tailored, corporate style. It is in fact a look I admire on many women, but one which I cannot pull off. The button-down, collared shirts never fit quite right or stayed smoothly inside the pants for more than five minutes. Everyone else looked neat, tidy, and together, while I was a crumpled mess before I got to my car. Once again, I stopped wearing that look. From now on I intend to stick with flowing lines, big sleeves, and loose tops . . . when I'm not in sweats.

Much love,
Marilyn

Marilyn

145

Otis

Dear Mildred,

I really looked forward to my trip to St. Louis because I knew that my friend Mildred was the best shopper in the whole world. You are the quintessential comparative shopper. As you have said, clothes are merely an outward expression of a person's inner creativity and artistry.

Thanks for helping me shop for my "mother of the groom dress." Bryant's wedding is an event at which I definitely want my outward and my inward to express the same thing. The dresses that I tried on certainly have the potential to express my own personal style.

"What is my personal style?" you ask.

A contemporary look, yet timeless in style. A color and tone becoming to my skin tones, comfortable to wear, with detail and character. Complementary to my large body and voluptuous breasts, capable of camouflaging a distended stomach and Afrocentric hips, proportionate to my stately 5 feet 1 inch stature, and economical. Finally, I must be able to wear this dress again and again for other occasions.

Please tell Pat and your "porcudawg" hello for me. I enjoyed being in your home and spending a few days in St. Louis. The highlight of my visit was visiting your office and meeting your associates. Please give them my best regards.

Will talk with you at the end of the month.

Love,
Otis

Dear Marilyn,

Recently I participated in a "Quiet Day of Meditation" at church. Our spiritual leader, a deacon from St. Peter's in Fernandina, guided us through several periods of meditation on the topic: Contemplative Prayer. Listening to recorded music from a monastery in Taizé, France, prepared us for our individual periods of contemplation and prayer. Except for the deacon we were all silent from 9:30 A.M. until 11:30 when we responded verbally during Communion.

At the end of the morning I experienced a glorious feeling of peace and contentment. These hours were a special time for my spiritual renewal. I know that in recent years you have been persistent in carving out time from your busy schedule to participate in a renewal seminar for extended periods of time. I could benefit from more frequent occasions for quiet times of renewal.

I am glad, however, that it is also possible to speak to and hear Him through the daily noises of our modern life. The hum of the computer, the ice maker drawing in water and spitting out ice, the telephone ringing, auto motors revving up, noises in the auto that speak "Your left door is open," or dogs barking in the yard. Noises like these are the environmental clutter of quiet.

More and more I sense a need to be silent, to experience the presence of God, and to listen to God. Because my world is so busy and noisy, silence must be choreographed, planned, and arranged. In recent years I applaud you for scheduling regular opportunities for renewal.

To help me in this perpetual quest for renewal, I

am reading some of the writing of Thomas Merton, a Catholic priest who lived a contemplative life. Currently, I am wading through Merton's <u>New Seeds of Contemplation</u>. I continue to use the music from Taizé to prepare my spirit and soul for fleeting moments of renewal.

Love,
Otee

Otis

Dear Lydia,

Next week the Year of the Rat begins. We have a very large Asian population here so Lunar New Year celebrations are big and colorful and noisy. It is great fun to celebrate new beginnings twice each year. Six weeks after I make New Year's resolutions I am reminded to consider again possibilities for the coming year. For this January 1, I wrote a short piece about my primary intention and I wish to share it with you:

Stay in the moment.
Be here, be aware of this current feeling, this
    thought.
Look around—
See every detail,
Every color,
Every shape,
Every facial expression,
Every body signal.
Listen carefully—
Hear the words,
And the space between the words.
Hear loud,
Soft,
And subtle
Sounds.
Be still when sitting.
Move directly when action is required.
Take care to do each in the right time.
Resist the lure of memories.
Resist the wish to replay old lines
As if they would change.

149

Take care of this time.
Ignore the call of future plans.
Use *now* for now.

Love,
Marilyn

Marilyn

150

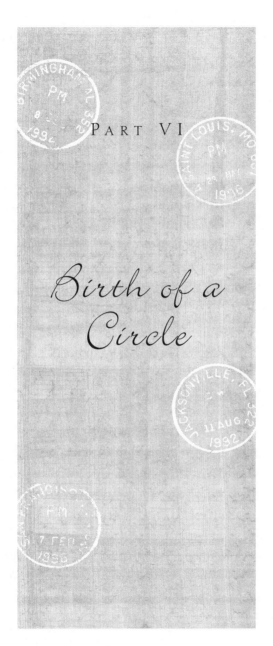

PART VI

Birth of a
Circle

Lydia

152

Dear Marilyn,

As I recount the experiences that led to the formation of our great circle, I delight in recalling the experiences of summer 1989 when my mother and I spent a few memorable days in San Francisco. Because of your gracious hospitality, my first trip to that beautiful city holds fond memories for me—the breathtaking scenery of the city, the refreshing air and wonder of nature in the open fields of wine country, the aura of elegance in your downtown abode, the unforgettable experience of reuniting with a college sister whom I had not seen for more than twenty years!

When you consider what had happened and what was happening in my life at that time, it's no wonder that summer 1989 was such a critical juncture for me. I had recently bowed out of, but had not recovered from, a relationship that turned out to be a bad investment of emotional energy; I had recently accepted a new position and was already having second thoughts about the decision; I had reached the minimum "service" requirement for retirement and had threatened to exercise the option "as soon as someone made me mad." I remember sharing with you two of the major reasons for my hesitancy at that point: affording good health insurance coverage while maintaining a comfortable lifestyle, and having sufficient financial resources to realize my lifelong dream of traveling until I grew tired of the practice. For me, your suggestion to pool our thinking with that of others who might share similar concerns was an excellent idea and one that I am happy that we pursued.

Love,

Lydia

Dear Lydia,

Plans for the minireunion are coming along. I have spoken with both Mildred and Otis and it looks like we can meet this spring.

I will be so happy to make plans for a career change. In fact, it is great just to imagine the possibility. These years at UCSF, especially the last seven, have been extremely difficult and anxiety-provoking. It's only when I focus on one patient and close out all the other circumstances associated with the hospital and academic environment that I can feel the least bit satisfied with my work. Patient care is the primary purpose of medicine and my primary interest, and yet that focus is so easily lost in the chaos of organizational politics. I have suffered the whole range of race- and gender-based problems. I have seen these issues addressed over and over, sometimes resulting in what I define as progress and sometimes not. I am bone-weary of it. I am becoming a bitter old witch and I don't like it one bit. Right now all I can think about is getting out, retiring early, leaving medicine. But what can I possibly do? I know that I desperately need to work with compatible people, but doing what? Our meeting will be my guide.

Take care, much love,

Marilyn

Marilyn

153

Dear Marilyn,

The late Alex Haley probably deserves some of the credit for sparking our initial decision to have a reunion with some special sisters. It must have taken your creative mind all of two minutes to decide that, while a reunion was a good idea, it should be a "minireunion" with a few people and it should have a specific focus (such as planning a retirement that would help us to accomplish the goals of continuing to make a meaningful contribution of service and providing supplementary retirement income). It probably took you no more than sixty additional seconds to identify the two people that would be invited to join. Following an "exploratory chat" with Otis, the rest is history.

I've never shared this with any of you, but I quietly questioned the compatibility of the four of us; I yielded to your wisdom because I realized that since you had been much closer than I to both Mildred and Otis during the years since our undergraduate days at Talladega, you must have known them well enough to know that it might work. I approached that first meeting with excitement and skepticism and was pleasantly surprised to find that we seemed to make an ideal combination. We were enough alike, and sufficiently different, to constitute a good team. While we don't seem to be moving fast enough for any of us (and I accept my share of the responsibility for that), I continue to look forward to the reinvigoration (and the laughs) that I get at our meetings and during our monthly conference calls.

Love,
Lydia

Dear Lydia,

It is truly amazing how my life has turned around. I feel like I've moved from a midlife mental mess to something approaching clear vision. When you and your mother visited, I was totally focused on how miserable I was. All my daydreams centered on how I could retire as early as possible. All my reading and studying about possibilities had generated information but no direction. I did learn that whom I worked with was much more important to me than what the job or venture turned out to be.

I was thrilled when you listened and suggested we get a group together. I vividly remember walking down the main street in Yountville, talking about your Miss Jane Pittman monologue, and your saying we should be able to figure out something for ourselves. It was your sympathy and understanding of my concerns and your willingness to move to the next level of planning that gave me inspiration and hope. The sun was bright that day, we had our fill of delicious Italian food, and I felt hopeful for the first time in a long time.

We had our first meeting in May 1990. I truly never had so much fun!! I was reminded of our days at Talladega, but felt so much freer, easier, and appreciative of the laughter and camaraderie. The brainstorming went well and when the visit was over, I had faith that my dream could come true. It had become a bigger and stronger dream, shared with three other dreamers.

Much love,
Marilyn

Marilyn

155

Dear Otis,

Each year since 1989, I have had unexpected changes in my life: new or changing job responsibilities, as well as changing feelings about the job itself; continued struggles to heal myself of the emotional scars left by what I considered my first real "rejection"; physical problems relating to my lower back and my gums; constant battles with my craving for chocolate chip cookies and other sinfully delicious food items and the resulting skyrocketing of my weight to unprecedented heights; combined with the need to remain positive enough to provide moral support for my "physically inconvenienced" mother.

On a much brighter note, I experienced the joy of becoming a grandmother on November 7, 1990, and you have some idea how my sanity has been gradually slipping away since that day. In many ways, being a grandmother has helped to compensate for other losses in my life, but having supportive friends and a newfound team of "significant others" has played a special role in my recovery. In other words, our circle has been, and continues to be, important to me. I can't imagine what my life would be like now if you girls had not happened <u>back</u> into it when you did. Whatever you do, don't ever leave me again.

Love,
Lydia

Dear Otis,

As I sit here on my 56th birthday—that is, eighteen years old in spirit and desire with thirty-eight years' experience—I find myself reflecting on August 1989. This is a "biggie" in my life because it reminds me of a birth. Now don't get any strange ideas; I am talking about the birth of an idea.

After the confusion of child-rearing years, I now find myself trying to channel my energy in the direction of old interests that I put on the back burner while James III and Roger Lindsay were growing up and demanding all of my waking hours. Each time I dialogue with our group I am reminded that there is more to life than sitting around mulling over the empty nest syndrome.

It is a pleasure looking upward with three great women who remind me of three towering oaks that are still producing brilliant ideas. We are facing the challenges of our growing years together with an understanding and concentration of the mind. With the group, I am always reminded to understand the things beyond my control and not take everything so seriously. This is always easier said than done, but it seems that when more than one person is saying it, it sounds like music to the ears. It enables me to hold on to courage and hope and not let doubt discourage me from doing anything I aspire to do. My thanks and compliments to you. For without friends and loved ones, my world would be nothing.

The periodic round robin meetings have provided me an opportunity to share some bittersweet physical and psychological changes of an aging body. By comparison and support from my three sisters, I

Mildred

can accept these changes as being part of another phase of life.

I am very lucky to have a support system to ease my frustrations. Life goes on as we continue to march to the beat of our own drummer.

Sisterly,
Mildred

Mildred

158

Dear Marilyn,

I don't know if you are aware, but you have personally provided inspiration for me in a number of ways. Our conversation in summer 1989 about smoking and your success in giving up the habit provided continued motivation for me in wanting and maintaining freedom from the habit for the past three years; your tips on exercise and the relationship between weak abdominal muscles and lower back problems led to my establishing a regular walking program (even though I became a "dropout" over a year ago); your cosmopolitan views on living and loving have helped me to reevaluate my own experiences; and the gentle way that all of you provide support and positive reinforcement has helped me not only to feel better about myself, but also to gain strength for the task of helping others to "celebrate themselves." (I'm still working on the "younger man" and the "nonblack" bit.) In a future missive, I will share some specific ways that I think the women of our circle have helped me to deal with problems as they have arisen since 1989 . . . most recently, the prayers that are buffering my mother for her back surgery tomorrow. I owe all of you a debt of gratitude for being a vital part of my life and I look forward with great anticipation to even more benefits of our union in the years to come. I love you—each one of you.

Love,
Lydia

Lydia

Dear Mildred,

Thank you for your wonderful, thought-provoking letter. I have enjoyed reading each of the letters from my wonderful sisters in the circle. Now it is my special privilege to write my reflections to you in this letter describing what was going on in my life before our circle.

The seeds of our circle were probably first sown in the fall of 1954 when you, Lydia, Marilyn, and I joined the Talladega College family. Actually, the seeds were sown earlier in 1953 when I first met Flora Lydia Lewis through the state 4-H Club meeting. Maybe it was even earlier, because Lydia's mom and my mom knew each other through the State Federated Women's Clubs. Through the years, we have managed to keep in touch via letters, telephone calls, and occasional visits. I have always known you were there for me and I have tried to be there for you. Of course, from Talladega in 1954 to San Francisco in 1989 there's LOTS OF STUFF BETWEEN.

I was excited when Marilyn called to invite the three of us to meet in San Francisco to explore ideas about our futures. Her call came at a time when my life seemed to be perched on a fulcrum of introspection and change. Marilyn's call gave reality to the persistent conversations I had recently been carrying on with myself about life, the meaning of life, and the future. Responding to that call was one of the wisest moves I ever made.

Love,

Otis

Dear Marilyn,

Happy New Year! Thanks to you, I will know enough about wines when I return to San Francisco to have a real appreciation for a trip to wine country. I was pleasantly surprised to receive the <u>Complete Wine Course</u> and to know that you thought enough of my interest to send it. Thanks so much. I will especially enjoy tasting as I read.

The snapshots are a couple of good reminders of your great hospitality last summer and the breathtaking sights in San Francisco.

My love life has had no improvement since I saw you. As a matter of fact, it has deteriorated even more. I finally told him that I wanted out, but the decision hasn't helped me to feel any better. I'm really not sure at this point whether I'm affected more by the decision (and subsequent decline in his attention to me) or by the inevitable admission that I <u>failed</u> with him. (Apparently I don't handle rejection well.) We still talk occasionally (even go to lunch or dinner sometimes) but the void is still there. Enough!!

About our spring fling. Otis told me that March is bad for Mildred. How about Easter weekend?

I spent the week before Christmas on a cruise with several family members. Luckily, it was the coldest week in Birmingham that we have had in years. Remind me to tell you about my son's visit to a nude beach. It was hilarious (his story, that is).

Let me know about Easter.

Love,
Lydia

Lydia

Otis

Dear Marilyn,

By the time I spoke with you in 1989 regarding the possibility of coming to San Francisco, I was beginning to enjoy the newfound freedom from motherhood. Since Bryant was in his freshman year at Birmingham Southern, I no longer had to be in place for his anticipated arrival home or emergency phone calls, nor did I have to monitor homework, chores, etc. Finally I believed that he was well on his way to accomplishing one of my major life goals—to see him educated and able to support himself. With Bryant having one foot out of the nest I felt ready to refocus my priorities.

Another issue I was dealing with in 1989 was adjusting to Jacksonville which was, after five years, less than I desired. For the first time in my life, making friends was extremely more difficult than in any other place that I have moved (and I have moved a lot). On a couple of occasions, when friendships were beginning, my emerging friends moved out of town, across town, or out of the country. These losses were not only painful but made me more reluctant to invest time and energy in developing new relationships.

In 1989, the thought of retirement, in the true sense of the word, seemed entirely alien to me. But I longed for a time when I could consider a second career. Doing this with some of my long-lasting friends was an intriguing thought. Our first weekend together was highly therapeutic for me. In the process, we have woven a tapestry of support for each other that has exceeded my wildest dreams. The group has encouraged me to dream dreams and explore a reservoir of untapped potential—potential that I hope will be resurrected to keep us involved until that time when we find a project that will excite us equally. I will pause here before I get redundant.

Love,

Otis

Otis

163

Lydia

Dear Marilyn,

It's amazing how the creative juices seem to flow so well in San Francisco. Is it the moderate weather? The water? The enthusiasm for life that is seemingly shared by people who live in (and <u>love</u>) San Francisco? The healthy habits that dominate? The healthful foods that seem more abundant there than anywhere I've been? Or is it <u>you</u> and your supportive spirit?

Whatever it is, I would not complain if we decided to meet in San Francisco once each year . . . at least until our project has reached fruition. We seem to jell so well out there—this time especially. As I told Mildred, I had begun to sense that we were drifting and fast becoming a trio rather than a foursome, and the retreat in San Francisco brought us together again. At last our circle seemed together again and it felt really good. Getting back home and back to the usual day-to-day routine always seems to stall things for a while, but the San Francisco air makes it all right again. As usual, you were a terrific hostess and I enjoyed the days that we spent together. You planned such a perfect blend of all the things that we know are vital to our mental health: healthful foods, clean water, exercise, meditation, rest, work, and fun. Now if I would just keep the momentum going at home.

See you in Jacksonville in November. I expect to be renewed (again) after vacationing in New England in October. Sure wish you could join me.

Love,
Lydia

Dear Mildred,

All day I have been thinking about the events of my summer. Seeing you, Marilyn, and Lydia was, as usual, loads of fun. Each of our meetings has been especially memorable. The June meeting in San Francisco was the very best. I do believe that we clicked as a team . . . no, as a sisterhood.

First, I must say thank you to the entire group for being my support at Chris and Lynn's wedding in Stockton. The presence of our circle provided that support that only could be generated by thirty-nine years of friendships. I realize that each of you endured major sacrifices to share this event with us. Marilyn gave up the comfort and coolness of San Francisco to drive to Stockton in the deadly summer heat which she loathes; Lydia gave up the opportunity to attend a few dozen meetings in Birmingham; and of course you, my dear sister, gave up a day of shopping. I do appreciate each of you in a very special way.

Of equal importance, I felt that you joined the group in both a physical and spiritual way. Because you had not attended the last meeting, I was feeling that the group might be moving in a direction that perhaps you could not fully endorse. I was wrong. You joined with such enthusiasm, wit, and insight that I am now truly excited in a new way about our adventure.

I am planning for our next gathering with great joy and excitement.

Love,
Otis

Otis

Dear Marilyn,

Roger called from Saudi Arabia on Sunday morning at 3:00 A.M. (12 noon Saudi's time.) He says he is fine. Thank God! Out of all the letters and packages that have been mailed to Roger in Saudi Arabia, he has received only your letter. Your letter was received on a day he was feeling exhausted and homesick. It gave him encouragement.

The Persian Gulf War has taken its toll on me both mentally and physically. I have lost ten pounds, which I could afford to lose, but I certainly did not plan to lose them through stress and strain. My hair is falling out, and I don't sleep very well. Now, mind you, these could be senior citizen symptoms, but I didn't notice this syndrome until Roger went to war. I can now identify with my mother's plight, for she had two sons go to war. My oldest brother, Jake, fought in World War II. Jack was in the Korean conflict. Both volunteered for the military at very young ages. Roger decided to join the reserve unit of the U.S. Marine Corps after college graduation. I do not understand his rationale. I am beginning to feel that I am being revisited by the ghost of years past. At one point in my life, I was so proud of my father, who told us stories of his courageousness in World War I, that I dreamed of joining the military after high school to continue the family tradition. It was only a passing fantasy for me, but Roger actively pursued my dream. What can I say?

I am trying to be patient and calm. I am putting all of my faith in God. I am confident that Roger will be safe. Roger knows that he is blanketed in the love and peace of God. This I know will be supportive energy, which will provide spiritual strength in a time of uncertainty.

Today, I was moved to pay a special tribute to <u>all</u> of those special military heroes who have chosen to defend the rights of others. I was impressed with the concerted effort of the parents, students, and teachers at our school to bake cookies, send letters, and launch balloons with special supportive messages to "Any Soldier." I was touched deeply by the outpouring of love and concern.

Dear friend, I am hurting inside. I am saying my prayers faithfully, and meditating every day and night.

I thank God for the true friendships that have sustained me during my trials and tribulations.

Thank you, Marilyn, for being there when I truly needed you.

Mildred

167

Love,
Mildred

Dear Mildred,

Please accept my sincere apology for speaking harshly to you last week. It was one of those times when I was too attached to being right and unwilling to acknowledge my error. Pride remains a demon to fight now as much as it was when I was young. So often I have blinded myself to the many different ways of looking at an issue by feeling that it was necessary to defend my initial stand. I truly respect your opinion and I resolve to listen carefully to what you offer.

I am still very busy with the remodeling project in Sebastopol. It appears that they will finish on time as promised, which is a rare occurrence. I will be so happy! It has been a real strain, much more difficult than I anticipated. Sometimes I feel like no one listens to me, especially about small details. Next time I'll know to put every light bulb on the blueprint and check all the orders for correct color. On the positive side, the workmanship is superb. I hope we will decide to meet there for a work session next year.

Take care.

Love,
Marilyn

Dear Marilyn,

Your letter of apology was well received today.

Thank you very much.

I admire your personal accomplishments and will continue to preserve an open mind on all debatable questions, like who is right or who is wrong. I have always considered it a mark of superior minds to disagree without being disagreeable; always keeping our long-standing friendship under complete control.

May I pause at this moment and reflect on the bond we created years ago? I can never replace your good deeds with a simple disagreement. Your words of consolation through my sorrow and tears will outshine any disagreement we may encounter. I have counted on your ability to remember each birthday, all holidays, and special occasions (sharing and caring), always rethinking a misunderstanding and sorting through the details, no matter what your ego says; in the end, you always apologize if you feel you are at fault.

I look with pride and admiration at the natural way in which you have weathered the minor complaints from me. Our disagreements have made me a stronger individual. We have shared a friendship that has grown deeper through the years. Through it all, I have learned that a true friendship must weather many storms and be filled with precious give-and-take moments.

Enjoy your trip to Sun Valley. Give Pinkie my best regards.

Love,

Mildred

Dear Lydia,

My thoughts are drawn to Washington. I can imagine you and all the "Degans" having a GRAND time. I'm sitting on the deck in Sebastopol and though part of me wishes to be in D.C., a tired and weary part is grateful for the rest and quiet here. My roommate Gloria called last week to see if I was going to the reunion.

The meeting of our circle last month was truly wonderful. As impossible as it seems, the meetings are becoming more productive and inspiring each time. Now I feel we are becoming a very cohesive working unit. The personal benefits for me continue to unfold and the collective creativity is gaining strength. There must be wondrous benefits in laughter. I am especially grateful for having a laugh at myself a time or two. You were so perceptive to pinpoint my growing rigidity. Somehow I must be mindful of the great wisdom in flexibility. I consider myself to be very flexible and accepting of ideas and differing styles, and have totally overlooked the ordinary day-to-day patterns I have established. Living habits become easily entrenched, especially since I need not consider anyone's needs or preferences except my own.

The talent and abilities that you, Mildred, and Otis continue to unveil are impressive. I look forward to each letter and phone call. I am totally convinced that we have something to offer others and putting it out into the world will bring us many rewards.

Take care, much love,

Marilyn

Marilyn

170

Dear Lydia,

What a difference a telephone call makes when one is in a depressed mood! I don't know whether you sensed I was having a gray day during our conference call tonight, but mental telepathy seemed to have put you in tune with my feelings. When you dialed me back immediately and hooked me up in conversation with your mother, I cherished that moment. Your mother's inner strength helped me to weather my private emotional storm. As a matter of fact, after talking to you, I closed my <u>emotional bank</u> and went to bed.

This is a special thank-you for being a perceptive human being and heeding my unspoken call for help. I cherish the friendship I have developed with you, Otis, and Marilyn. What a welcome relief to talk woman-to-woman to vent my frustrations. My good friends have served an important purpose in my life. Without my female friends, I would live my senior status in a male-dominated bubble—two sons and a husband. What I am trying to say is our circle has become the fabric of my life.

A good friend remarked to me that I am fortunate to have three good female friends that I have been in touch with throughout college to the present. She remarked what a rarity it is to stay in touch for forty-plus years and not get burned out. She said that she doesn't have any female confidantes. Her experiences have had a few disastrous endings—jealousy and irreparable differences. At that moment, I began to count my blessings "threefold."

Love,

Mildred

171

Lydia

Dear Mildred,

I can't wait to share with Mama your kind words about the conversation that you had with her in our three-way chat last week. She truly is an inspiration to most people who know her, and I should not be surprised that you picked that up about her without ever having met her face-to-face. I may have told you before but Mama has suffered from a physical "inconvenience" since the turn of the '70s. In varying degrees of severity, she has endured pain, a series of operations, and an endless list of doctors to address a myriad of problems including osteoarthritis, nerve collapse, and gastrointestinal trouble. In spite of her woes, she has managed to maintain a smile amid adversity and somehow manages to cheer those who come to give her a boost. Sometimes I get so irritated with her when she starts to doubt her abilities, because as I have told her many times, she thinks better when she's napping than most people do when they're wide awake.

In going through some mementos recently, I ran across a letter that she wrote to me in 1988 that reveals some of the essence of her inner strength. It was uplifting for me to read it again and I thought you might enjoy reading it as well. I think it should be published in somebody's book of inspirational thoughts. Don't you agree?

Love,
Lydia

Dear Lydia,

Thanks very much for the dinner; it was delicious. You couldn't have done it at a better time. I had reneged on cooking. It seems that I'm losing my touch.

Last week I felt that I had reached my rope's end and I ran across an old <u>Daily Message</u> in which the writer stated that life is fired at us point-blank; we cannot put off living until we are ready. When faced with handicaps, we ask questions: Why? Why me? How long? This writer suggested that with our hurts we can become either a pool or a channel. We become pools when we permit self-pity to take control; then we become a part of the problem. But we can become a channel for ministry to others who need comfort. What we have suffered can equip us to help others who suffer as we do. I think I also heard something you have said to me many times—that you think I am an inspiration to others. I took another look at the rope and decided to knot it and hang in a while longer. I don't want to be a pool of self-pity.

Thanks for the Scrabble game. It means so much for those you love dearly to take some time with you. I realize that you are very busy. I am so glad God has endowed you as He has and I am more proud that you listen to His guidance. With His guidance, I think you have been a good mother, and I pray that your love, patience, courage, and understanding will prevail even into grandparenthood. I know how we can anticipate and feel that things move so slowly, but our love for the Lord helps us to trust Him and know that in His infinite wisdom, all things happen for the best. You and Judson have had the greatest adjustment of the family, and I am proud and grateful to God that

Mom

He is leading and directing you. I pray His choicest blessings. You are a channel of His love for sure.

Well, I just wanted to share with you that I have a renewed zest for living and loving with my family and trying to know and do my Father's will.

God bless you and keep you.

Love,

Mom

Mom

174

Dear Mildred,

Thank you for my wonderful week vacationing at your beautiful home in Kernersville. As you know, I needed the rest and relaxation that only the "Patterson Resort" could offer. After a summer filled with numerous stressful events, I needed rest. I felt so exhausted just before I left Jacksonville that I almost called to say I could not make the trip. Needless to say, I would have missed the rejuvenation that I always feel whenever you, Marilyn, Lydia, and I get together. Being with my sisters is always therapeutic.

Now, you will never believe what happened yesterday. One of my colleagues brought me a gift from Benin, Africa. It is the most beautiful piece of purple fabric that I have ever seen. Receiving this gift was proof—no, a "sign"—that my title for the book is indeed right. I will fashion this fabric into the prettiest purple dress that you have ever seen. I guess I was looking for affirmation that "Purple Dresses and Green Tigers" is a good title for the book. Now I have it.

Charles was pleased to spend some quality time with Pat. He really enjoyed the time, though brief, with Pat and the group. Thank you for inviting Harrell and Ivory over for dinner. It was an elegant and enjoyable evening. I hope you will remain in contact with them.

I am ecstatic about being back at work after such a wonderful vacation. At last I have the energy that I had lost over the past few weeks of the summer.

Hello to Ash from me.

Love,
Otis

Otis

Otis

Dear Lydia,

There are times when the "poor me" mood is upon us and we can be overwhelmed by the trouble we have to face. For this frame of mind, our circle has an infallible prescription. It is difficult to believe that the four of us met forty years ago and have shared our lives since that time. None of us ever dreamed that our friendship would carry us through the best of times and the worst of times.

We are more than friends to each other. You are the humorist, Marilyn is the advisor, Mildred is the confidante, and I am the counselor. We believe in emptying our minds of all thoughts but one—today and how to use it.

Our lives are shaped by our faith, unconditional support, and strength of purpose. No matter what, we do not forget each other. We are reminded by each letter and telephone conversation that there is more to life than sitting around engaging in a "pity party."

We listen without judging. Rather than shove advice down each others' throats, we offer gentle guidance. Sometimes we babble for hours and sometimes we just sit quietly and meditate. Sometimes we can't offer advice, but we can be the sounding board that assures us not to worry because everything will work out just fine. This is the real value of our special relationship.

Love,
Otis

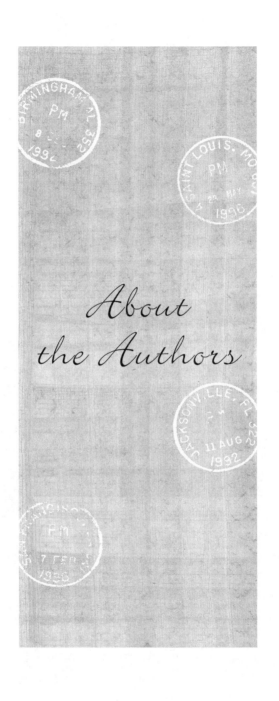

*About
the Authors*

Lydia Lewis Alexander

I had no idea when I met Mildred Lucas, Marilyn Hill, and Otis Holloway at Talladega College in September 1954 that we would still be friends more than forty years later or that we would be collaborating on a book! We all knew each other at Talladega—even did many things together—but none of us were ever roommates; none of us were especially "tight" in college, and I never lived in the same town or worked in the same place with any of them. Whoever termed the alumni "The Talladega Family" must have felt that special bond of friendship that was created among the students, because whenever Talladegans get together, they all act like lifelong friends and family.

Otis and I had met earlier at a statewide 4-H Club meeting, and our mothers had met through their federated club work on the state level. At Talladega, Otis had a clear advantage over the other freshmen because her roommate was not only her sister, but a junior who could show her the ropes. That may explain why Otis was our self-appointed guardian. I can see her autograph in my senior yearbook now: "I'm glad we're parting because you make me nervous. Don't hide your talent under a bushel." (I must admit that my adventurous nature was enough to make most people nervous, but I had a lot of fun!)

Over the years, Otis and I saw each other occasionally when she visited her sister in Birmingham, and when she (Otis) worked at the University of Alabama in nearby Tuscaloosa. Mildred and I got together at national meetings of our sorority, and Marilyn and I kept in touch through the mail. Otis and Charles's wedding in 1968 and our 25th Reunion weekend at Talladega in 1983 were the only times that all four of us were in the same city at the same time before our minireunion in 1990.

It was pure coincidence that Otis and I ended up in the same college major (history) and with the same career goal—becoming a lawyer. I don't know why she didn't pursue law, but I know what happened to me. I decided to get my teaching certificate so I would have something to "fall back on," as people used to say. I never really wanted to teach, even though there were several educators in my family. When we graduated, I decided to teach for a couple of years to earn enough money to support myself in law school, and fell in love with the profession. When I'm in the company of friends who have entered law as a second profession, I frequently refer to myself as a "frustrated would-be lawyer." Although I would not consider pursuing law at this point, it is an unfulfilled dream of mine.

I remember Mildred and Marilyn as college marshals, the ushers for special events and Sunday worship that we were all required to attend. I don't know if their role as marshals made required chapel more palatable for them, but I do know that singing in the choir made it more palatable for me. I never did like being told what to do. I always wanted the freedom to make my own choices. Somehow, the idea of going to "chapel" to sing in the choir made attendance seem more like a personal choice than a requirement imposed by the college.

My freshman year was catch-up time for me. When I discovered that my class was heavily populated with valedictorians and salutatorians of their high-school graduating classes, I knew I had some catching up to do. Many of them were products of private schools (Otis and Marilyn were among that group) and had been exposed to what some people thought was a much better education than was available in the public schools. Fortunately, our professors treated us all as if we were products of exclusive private schools, and we were forced to perform as if we were.

When Otis, Marilyn, and I pledged Alpha Kappa Alpha (AKA) in the fall of 1955 (Mildred pledged in 1956), I began a lifelong career of "service" to my community. My life at Talladega was filled with extracurricular activities then, just as it is now filled with an array of service activities from the school board to the sorority. Maybe all those "lessons" I had in my youth were worth my parents' investment. I had lessons in voice, piano, modeling, dancing, and drama and had started appearing on stage at an early age. At Talladega, I sang in the choir, traveled with the modern dance troupe and the Little Theater, and even became a cheerleader for the basketball team. You might say I squeezed classes in between activities then like I squeeze work in between community activities now.

At Historic Canaan Baptist Church, I am a deaconess, a member of a couple of choirs, and a founder and first president of our kindergarten advisory board. For several years, I worked with the local Sickle Cell Foundation, serving in several capacities, including president of the board. Otis's sister, Florence, teases me about "running everything in town except Delta Sigma Theta." My brother recently remarked that I was the most skillful time manager that he had ever seen. (He must have observed me squeezing forty-eight hours of work into a twenty-four-hour day.)

Talladega College didn't have a football team when we were there; that might explain why there were so few men on campus. The number of men at the college was so low that our dorm counselor suggested that those of us who had boyfriends should give them up after a couple of months so the other women could have a chance to date. I didn't know about the others, but I wasn't about to sacrifice my boyfriend so he could enhance some other girl's self-esteem.

Life on the campus of Talladega College was a striking contrast to life in the surrounding community. At the college, we were black, white, red, yellow, African, Asian, and European, yet we all managed to get along with (and respect) each other. Out in the city, segregation and racial prejudice abounded and most people probably didn't even care that the court decision banning segregated schools had been handed down. Fortunately, the faculty and administration at the college provided what we needed within the confines of the campus. We frequently had nationally recognized artists and speakers such as Leontyne Price and Martin Luther King, Jr., appear on campus. They even showed movies on campus, so we didn't have to subject ourselves to the back door and balcony in the local theater.

Sixteen years of my life had passed when I entered Talladega, but until that day in 1954, I had spent my life in Bessemer, Alabama, a small town of about 35,000 people located thirteen miles southwest of Birmingham. It was on August 21, 1938, at two o'clock in the afternoon, that my mother, Flora Laird Lewis (see "Inspiration" on page 172), gave birth to her second child. She and my dad, Clinton E. Lewis (see "Struggling for Strength" on page 60), had married in June of 1936 and had started their family with a son, Clinton, Jr., in March of 1937. With my birth, the family was complete, so they thought. To their surprise, I became the middle child in October 1941, when my sister Gwen (see "Sounding Boards" on page 34) was born. As a result of this addition to the family, I grew up between a brother whose chauvinism was in full bloom at an early age, and a gifted sister who was the teacher's pet at school and the favorite child at home. Of course Mom and Dad always denied that they played favorites, but who wouldn't favor a child who never caused parents a headache? Clint and I caused our share of headaches, but Gwen was sweet and quiet and studious and virtually always did as she was told.

Until somebody's research described "Negro" children as "disadvantaged," I had always thought that our family was typical. My dad was a machine operator in the local steel plant and my mother was a schoolteacher. We lived in a neighborhood that remained predominantly white until the '90s. Now, my mother is the lone African American in her block who has lived there since the '40s. The others have either died or moved away.

I was named after my Daddy's Aunt Lydia, whose

even-temperedness was an example for all of us. Not only did we never hear her raise her voice when we visited her, but Daddy's cousin, Connie, who lived with her for several months, said she never saw Auntie Lydia lose her temper either. I adored Auntie Lydia and her daughter, Mary Ellen. Both of them were teachers in Jefferson County, and Cousin Mary Ellen was married to the leading "colored" physician in Bessemer. Her son, George, was the first "Ivy League" product of the family. After attending a public elementary school here, George earned his high-school diploma at Phillips Academy in Andover, Massachusetts, and his undergraduate degree at Yale before entering Case Western Reserve University to pursue his medical degree. A top-notch internist in California for several years, he died of cancer in 1990, depriving the world of another wonderful person. What a legacy he left for his sons.

I always knew that the white children in my neighborhood went to a different school, but I didn't know until much later that the books and lockers that we received were the throwaways from the white school when new ones were bought for the white children. Until then, I thought the major difference in our schools was that the races were simply "housed" in separate facilities. I was aware that although there was a high school two blocks from our home, we had to travel across town to get to the "colored" school, but I thought for a long time that we were getting the same education. Our parents tried hard to protect us from the surrounding racist environment to ensure that we felt good about ourselves. Because of their efforts, I didn't grow up bitter and ready to harm the first white person who came in close contact with me.

I didn't have a regular playmate during my early

years. Clint played with the older guys (both white and black) in the neighborhood, and my sister was too young to "run with me." After starting school at five and advancing a grade by going to school during a couple of summers, I was always the youngest in my class, so I didn't need an even younger sister tagging along with me. I was busy trying to look and act older, so I sought the company of older children. With each passing year, I find myself wishing that I had held on to that youth a little longer.

My mother began her teaching career in 1943, after my brother and I had started school. As a teacher's daughter, I lived in a glass house and was watched constantly by neighbors, teachers, and even family members. We always knew we were going to college, so we knew better than to make bad grades. I only had a few privileges (because our parents were so strict), but those few would have been lifted if my grades had not been good. My biggest problem was talking in class, so I learned this lesson when I made $\underline{C}$ in Conduct.

My teenage years were trying times because I was always chronologically two years younger than my peers. I envied their freedom to do things I couldn't, and I expended a lot of emotional energy trying to prove that I could do what they did, not realizing at the time that most of what they did wasn't worth imitating. I must admit that my driving force to maintain honor-roll status was not motivated by a desire to learn as much as by my desire to please my parents. It wasn't until I found myself in a class of high achievers at Talladega College that I realized I had not been intrinsically motivated to learn for the sake of learning.

I first dated the man I married when I was a senior in

high school. J.T. (see "Pondering Loneliness" on page 42) had returned home from the Korean conflict where he had spent a few years in the Air Force. Being the handsome and debonair veteran that he was, he probably dated a different girl every other night, but I had the distinction of having his company on Wednesday and Sunday nights, the official nights for girls to "receive company."

When I went away to college, I dated other guys (was even engaged for a brief period to one of them) and J.T. dated other young women. We finally decided to seal the relationship with marriage in December 1961, three and a half years after my college graduation. Our marriage ended abruptly after nineteen years when he died in a tragic accident. Less than two months after our son had enrolled as a freshman at Talladega College, I was thrust into single parenthood, grasping desperately for ways of surviving without my right hand and trying to compensate for my son's loss of a father. I know I made a lot of mistakes trying to be both father and mother, but, thank God, Judson survived my blunders and grew to become a fine young man. I sometimes wish we had given him a sister or brother, but when I suggested it in my 30th year, J.T. told me that I was "too old and nervous" by then.

J.T. was the youngest of ten children, eight of whom are still living. Since his death, the remaining brothers and sisters have continued to treat me as one of the family, and I feel so fortunate to share that bond with them and their wonderful sons and daughters. Not only do they (especially George) look after me, but they also share my pride in my son and my grandchildren. I only wish J.T. could have lived to enjoy Judson as an adult and experience the great joy of our grandchildren.

Several of the folks in the community thought that J.T. and I weren't a good match because he was not a college graduate. Clearly, they were making the mistake of equating degrees with sense and maturity. When the marriage succeeded, some of those same skeptics said later, "I always knew they would make it. They were such an ideal couple." I'm sure if our marriage had failed, many of those same skeptics would have said, "I'm not surprised. They were misfits from the beginning." People had us divorced each time I earned a degree. They didn't know that he was the real reason for my going further in school and it was largely due to his encouragement and support that I was able to accomplish those goals. J.T. taught me a lot about people, especially in developing the strength to not be concerned about what they said.

In 1972 I earned a doctorate and began a career in university teaching that has continued to this day. J.T. had entered Auburn to complete his baccalaureate degree while I was completing the doctorate, and we enrolled Judson in the public schools there for that two-year period. After J.T.'s graduation from Auburn, we resumed life in Bessemer in 1974. Later that year, I joined the University of Alabama at Birmingham faculty and spent the next twenty-two years in teaching and administration.

Judson, Jr., is now sharing his life with his wife, Yolanda, and their two children, Judson III ("Theo") and Ashlee, in Huntsville, Alabama. I often dream of retiring and moving closer to them so I can enjoy my grandchildren on a regular basis. For the time being, I have the satisfaction of knowing that Judson lives near his godmother, Nell, and her husband, Fred, who provide a wonderful support system for the family. As often as Judson talks to my sister Gwen and her husband, Harllee, you wouldn't think they live in D.C. He thinks nothing of calling them and engaging in a lengthy discussion of the latest developments in politics. (We all thirst for stimulating conversation.) Gwen and Harllee, Judson and Yolanda, and I are all graduates of Talladega and Gwen's son Fred is a student there now. Her daughter, Linda, broke away from tradition and earned her undergraduate degree from University of the District of Columbia and her master's from Trinity. When my mother and I go to Washington, we can see most of our immediate family because my brother, Clint, a financial wizard, lives in nearby Silver Spring, Maryland, with his partner and wife, Zona. His daughter, Ava, recently left Baltimore and relocated out West, so he doesn't get to see his beautiful granddaughters as often as he'd like to, I'm sure. We didn't meet our half-brother, Frank, until I was in high school, but we have made up for many of those lost years by traveling together and visiting each other in person and by phone. He and his wife, Mae, recently gave up the snow in Michigan and retired to Florida, where they live on a golf course. When I asked Frank what he does with his time now that he's retired, he responded "absolutely nothing . . . and I don't start that until twelve o'clock." They are absolutely ecstatic over becoming first-time grandparents in 1995, the year that their son, Eric, the new father, turned forty.

My father's sudden death in 1976 was a devastating blow to all of us (see "Devastating Losses" on page 52). Because of my mother's physical condition, she was so sure that Daddy would outlive her. After all, he came away from his physical every year with a clean bill of health, while she had fought a number of physical problems since the late 1960s. When she realized she was alone and "crippled," she turned to God, gathered up her inner strength, and rose to the occasion. Since she retired on disability in the late '70s, she has continued to be involved in the community. When it is difficult for her to get out, people come to her so they can take advantage of her brilliant mind. Although she is in a wheelchair now, she wears a perpetual smile, is mentally alert, and quite an inspiration to others.

Holidays are the hardest times for us. When I was a child, we always had such fun on holidays because we had a large family to share those occasions with. We would always gather at the family home shared by two of my great aunts, Aunt Emma and Aunt Maggie, and their husbands, Uncle Jesse and Uncle Tommy. Aunt Baby and Uncle Charlie (later Uncle Randle) lived next door to them and my grandmother lived in the apartment over the garage. It was like a family compound where everybody gathered at Christmas and Thanksgiving. We had many other family meals there, but on Christmas and Thanksgiving, we shared talents and gifts and gave testimonies to God's goodness to each of us. My mother and my aunts spoiled me so much with their scrumptious holiday meals that I never bothered to bake a turkey or prepare any of the other traditional holiday meals. I think I was over forty before I baked a turkey, and I have never cooked chitterlings to this day.

The saddest thing about the bustling family holidays is that they ended. Over the years, the great aunts and uncles died away and the cousins all moved away, leaving our family smaller with each passing year. With Uncle John's passing last December, the family is now reduced to my mother and me. For several years, we spent major holidays out of town visiting my sister and brother or on family vacations together. With my mother's mobility further reduced, we now face more lonely holidays at home.

It was summer of 1989 when I started to ponder seriously the idea of retiring. In a way, you could say that *Wearing Purple* was conceived that summer when I visited Marilyn on a vacation that my mother and I had taken to the West Coast (see "Birth of a Circle" on page 152). During the past few years of our biannual meetings and monthly telephone calls, we have enjoyed many hours of reflections of the years since 1954 and have embedded some of those memories in the letters found in the pages of *Wearing Purple*. I hope that in reading these letters, you will gain a fraction of the enjoyment that we experienced in writing them.

$\mathcal{M}arilyn \ \mathcal{H}ill \ \mathcal{H}arper$

My high school principal in Seneca, South Carolina, the little town where I grew up, convinced Daddy and Mother that I needed a stronger academic background than his school provided. Mother had dreams of New England prep schools. Daddy had nightmares about their cost. I feared I didn't have the right clothes for New England. We all decided that Mather Academy, right there in South Carolina, was a fine school and excellent choice.

My first day there I was welcomed at the entrance by Arneta, who was to become my best high-school friend. She was a warm and generous person and I instantly knew we would get along and Mather would be fun. I was very lucky to spend two years at Mather. The end of May 1954 came too soon for me. I wasn't ready to leave that place forever, and it would definitely be forever. I knew in my heart I'd never see most of my classmates again. Tears, endless tears, streamed down my puffy face.

"Good-bye." "Give me a hug." "Where are you going to college?" Get dressed. Finish packing. I didn't want to pack. I didn't want this to be the last day. I was safe here. I was happy here. My friends were fun. I knew I was welcome in their rooms. I knew they would share everything with me. Boarding school. Dormitory life. Each girl in a small circle. Each circle linked to the other. So much laughter. Such anguish over boys. Whispers. Secrets. "Who sneaked off campus?" "Who met her boyfriend in the basement?" What did they do in the basement anyway? "Will the headmistress let one of us go to the bakery for one last chocolate cake?" I was never chosen to go off campus. That was okay. I got to take Neat and Billie to the drugstore for ice cream those Sundays when Daddy came to visit. I also went with the football team to all the away games. A cheerleader. A very conservative school. No legs showing when I jumped. I wore long full skirts and heavy letter sweaters. I hid behind the school bus to kiss my boyfriend after the games. He ran beautifully and made many touchdowns. I'd never see him again. More tears. Stop crying. Everyone will think you're silly. No one else is crying. After today I'll never let anyone see me cry. "Say good-bye to Ellen." I'll even miss quiet, shy Ellen. "Where is Harvey?" He said he would visit over the summer. I didn't believe him. Better say good-bye now. "What about Mrs. Benson?" I was a little afraid of the headmistress. Still, it seemed right to say good-bye properly. "Where is my camera?" I must get a picture of everyone today. Pose. Smile. How very grown-up we all looked in our caps and gowns. How could we be ready for college? How will I bear to go to a strange place in September? How can I sit all summer at home, not knowing what the new school will be like? "Get a picture of Helen." How lucky Helen was. A junior. One more year of fun. "Get in the car." One more snapshot. "It's a long drive home." One more hug. One last look. One last kiss. One smile through my tears.

My tears were unwarranted. At Talladega I found many lifelong friends. It was at Talladega that I felt truly at home and part of the community. I met Gloria the first day when we were assigned to be roommates and we remained roomies for four years. I fell in love with a wonderful guy the first week and we have remained friends ever since. He walked across the campus green with his head held high. Smooth, handsome, black hair, dark eyes, and a smile designed to dazzle. "That's the one for me," I thought, wondering how I would get his attention.

He was an upperclassman, there early to help with freshman orientation. He stopped and sat on the brick wall which bordered Battle Street. That street bisected the campus, dividing the girls' dorms, dining hall, and chapel from the academic buildings, student union, and boys' dorms on the north side. The wall was a perfect place for students to gather. It provided a great vantage point from which to watch comings and goings. It was hard to move around campus without being seen from the wall. I walked over to him.

"I'm Marilyn. Would you like to take me to the movie Friday night?"

"Sure."

I smiled brightly and walked on over to the science building. No further arrangements were necessary. All the boys came to Foster Hall to pick up their dates.

My date arrived barely on time. We sat high up in the balcony in what were to become our regular seats. I delighted in his easy manner and his well-established camaraderie with the male campus big shots. We held hands through the movie and went with everyone else for hamburgers and Cokes after the show.

On Sunday I was astonished when he sang the primary solo in chapel. He had a clear, strong tenor which threw notes high into the air and let them hang there for a while. His version of the Lord's Prayer brought tears to everyone's eyes.

"What's your major?"

"Humanities. It's nice and easy."

"I have to decide between biology and chemistry. Either one will work for medical school."

"Medical school? You?"

"Yes, me. I think I'll choose biology. That way I won't have to take calculus."

We spent four years together, off and on. During the "on" times we were constant companions, going everywhere together, eating hamburgers three times a day, except for fried chicken from Hipockets on Sunday. The "off" times meant dating others. NOT by mutual consent. We always wound up back together, embracing tenderly under a tree in front of Foster Hall.

"How's your senior project, Marilyn?"

"The cell culture didn't work, but Miss Taylor liked my ideas so it'll be all right."

"I'm starting grad school in Chicago."

"Chicago is fun. You'll have a great time and two years to figure out where to live afterward."

"I'm going back home to work with my Dad."

"You really want to go back there?"

"Yes. Dad has a good business. It makes sense. Let's get married."

"I don't want to live in a small town in the South."

"You haven't been to my hometown. How do you know?"

"They're all the same. I'm going to medical school. To Howard. Washington will be fun."

"I don't want my wife to be a doctor. I'll make enough money to take care of you."

"I know you will. That's not the point. You know I always planned to be a doctor."

"I thought you'd change your mind."

Talladega was the place where I started growing up. The campus community provided protection for the naive while affording opportunities to make difficult decisions. I joined Alpha Kappa Alpha and found my first circle of women friends. One year Otis was basileus and I was dean of pledges. We spent the summer writing back and forth about our wonderful plans for the sorority. We intended to make it the best year ever, with a lovely pledge line, fantastic social affairs, and many "worthwhile" activities.

Bridge games in the dorm were a favorite activity and I still keep in touch with Irby, who hosted many games. Lydia lived across the hall and was the better bridge player by far. She and I spent one afternoon smoking cigarettes, drinking Cokes, and constructing a list of the essential qualities our future husbands must possess. I didn't marry a "Degan," but the men of Alpha Phi Alpha became good friends and made me their sweetheart. Many of us vied for the honor of going home with Otis to Mt. Meigs. I felt like Mr. and Mrs. Holloway were my Alabama parents. Their big white house was welcoming. She was a fabulous cook. We didn't have to do any work. Mrs. Holloway was supersensitive to any signs of distress and ready with advice and comfort. Those were wonderful, fun, and exciting years, and I even got a good education squeezed in between activities.

My first fourteen years had been spent in a pleasant, small Southern town. I lived with my parents, Harold and Eugenia Hill, and my sister, Ercelle, in Seneca, South Carolina. My dad was a pharmacist. Sometimes the phone rang in the middle of the night. Daddy would get up and go to the drugstore to get medicine for some poor soul. I wondered why they couldn't get what they needed during the day. Many years later I learned that medical emergencies were frequent and hard to anticipate. "I'll be right there. Meet me at the drugstore." Whoever, whenever, Daddy would go. He spent his whole life in that store. Prescriptions filled, advice dispensed, seven days a week. He took Wednesday afternoon off, opened after church, and closed early on Sunday. Except for the two weeks every other year when we went to New York to watch the Brooklyn Dodgers play baseball, he was always right there. Many people checked with Daddy at the drugstore before going to the doctor. "What can you give me for this, Doc?" they'd ask. Daddy would suggest a remedy or tell them they should go next door to see Dr. Battle. He was always ready to help anyone and was loved by the whole town in return. We spoke little. I imagine how it would have been to share my thoughts and my worries, my successes and my difficulties, with him. Some gaps cannot be bridged. The gaps of perception were too wide for us.

Mother was tall and beautiful, distant and reserved, and very busy when I was young. Her activities had two areas of primary focus. The first was Daddy. The family schedule, menus, holiday plans, vacations, and any social activities were designed to suit his needs and desires. Her other passion was civic service. She belonged to the Methodist Women's Society, the NAACP, The Links, and many other women's service clubs.

She also enjoyed gardening. She grew massive amounts of tomatoes, green beans, peas, corn, squash, watermelon, and cantaloupes in our big backyard. The front yard was bordered with hydrangeas, and tall, graceful gladiolus lined both sides of the house. The summer weeks were marked off by her planting, weeding, and staking of beans and tomatoes. Summer storms were frequent and welcome, so weeding and hoeing were essential, but she didn't have to water. In late summer the back porch would fill with huge baskets of vegetables. She blanched them and packed them in pint and quart containers for freezing in the community locker plant. Since she didn't have fruit trees, she bought peaches in bushel baskets. We would sit on the porch peeling and slicing peaches for hours. These were also frozen, and we knew that winter desserts would be peaches and ice cream, peach pie, or peach and strawberry shortcake.

Late Sunday afternoons Daddy would close the drugstore and take us for a ride. Usually we visited my parents' friends in neighboring towns. If Daddy felt really good we'd go to Hendersonville, North Carolina. That was my favorite trip. Our little town is at the foot of the Blue Ridge Mountains, so wherever we drove I could see the mountains. But when we went to Hendersonville I was treated to the hills coming closer and closer until I was in the middle of tall pine trees. I loved the mountains and wildflowers and especially the trees. The Blue Ridge Mountains really do have a blue shimmer when seen from a distance. They look like slate-blue lumps of Silly Putty. I always sat in the left back seat behind Daddy, leaned my head against the car, and pretended I was going away with my one true love. His identity changed depending on which basketball star or classmate I was madly in love with at the time, but we always went far, far away from South Carolina.

My favorite place to imagine living was New York City. When I was six years old, Daddy went to New York without us. I begged and begged to go along and somehow got the idea that there wasn't enough money for my train ticket. So I gathered up pecans from the backyard and sat out on the sidewalk selling them to earn my fare. I packed my bags, made myself a lunch, and was totally devastated when Daddy left without me. For years afterward I dreamed of one day living in New York.

I am four years older than my sister Ercelle, which I assumed for most of our childhood gave me the right to offer opinions and advice. She called it bossy. She was the graceful athlete, but I had four years on her so I was pretty good at roller-skating before she tried to learn. I decided to tie a pillow around her waist and hips so that she wouldn't get hurt when she fell. Of course this threw her off balance and made skating more difficult. My advisory status ended at a very early age.

When I was eight years old, I spent two weeks with my Aunt Rheba in Atlanta. One day we went downtown on a bus. I climbed the steps and popped into the first empty seat. Aunt Rheba grabbed my arm, the bus driver yelled, "You know you can't sit there," and the other passengers snickered. I was humiliated, confused, and wondered what was wrong with me. It is a wonder that has recurred over the years.

I cannot remember a time when I didn't know that my Daddy wanted me to be a doctor. "Write the orders, don't follow them," he'd say. I considered the few other options available. I could be a teacher, nurse, dentist, lawyer, or housewife, my mother's clear preference. Teaching college-level biology was attractive, but I always came back to medicine as first choice. I enjoyed the thought of knowing what to do and how to help when someone was sick or hurt. I didn't realize how difficult medical school would be. There was constant pressure and a persistent fear of not being able to read enough, of failing the next exam. One of our freshman professors said to the assembled first-year class of eighty-eight men and twelve women that "you girls are just taking up space that should have gone to a man who would use his education and not just get married and have children." On the other hand, I loved living alone and being in charge of my own schedule, never mind that it consisted mostly of study time. Any moment stolen from reading for the next

day's classes felt delicious, and a short nap after dinner was heaven. I studied for exams in a small group of several classmates, sharing lecture notes and generally helping each other.

The summer before my wedding, Otis spent the summer with me. We shared my tiny one-bedroom apartment in Washington, D.C. I had just finished my second year of medicine and was doing an externship in pediatrics at Walter Reed Hospital. She was going to graduate school at Howard University. Our classmate and sorority sister Mildred and her friend Annie Mae would leave dormitory life and join us in the apartment on weekends. Mildred was very attractive, outgoing, and popular. One of her many admirers worked for a florist. He would send huge bouquets of flowers for her almost every weekend.

We had a great time sight-seeing, shopping, and generally doing what would now be called "hanging out." One Friday afternoon a gigantic arrangement of roses and lilies arrived for Mildred. It was exquisite. It probably had two dozen roses and nearly as many lilies. When Mildred arrived, she smiled slyly and said, "Where did you get the lovely flowers?" clearly assuming that they were hers. I said, "They're from Harry. Wasn't he nice to send them for no reason whatever?" She was crestfallen, mumbled something about thoughtfulness, and went on to speak about our weekend plans. I didn't tell her until Sunday evening that the flowers were really hers.

It was a summer of magic and laughter. Within a year, Mildred and I had each married and thus embarked upon the female journey: career and children and home and husband and civic duties, all to be managed simultaneously. At least Mildred did all these well. I eventually focused on career and children.

I married a medical school classmate, and my first son, Harry III, was born in South Bend, Indiana. Frank (whose name was later changed to Hill) was born two and a half years later in Iowa City, Iowa. Postgraduate training, small boys, and the Midwestern climate, both social and weather, combined to keep me busy making one adjustment after another. I was tired for ten years.

One summer when I was between baby-sitters, Otis came to my rescue. Her visit and help were a gift from heaven. I could not secure any days off since the medical establishment did not consider it an emergency when our sitter abruptly decided to leave. Her Iowa City visit was more work than fun for her, but I tried to make up for that during other visits. She has come to every place I have ever lived.

We spent several years in Fort Madison and Keokuk, Iowa. It was a time of challenge which finally got the best of me. Anyone would think I had it good. A big house on the best street in town, overlooking the marvelous Mississippi River, two beautiful boys, a modest but not overly taxing career, membership in the country club, invitations to whatever passed for social events in small-town Iowa. Security, position, and all the typical pieces of the American dream were in place. Yet I was miserable. I kept trying to figure out what was wrong with me. Why wasn't I happy? I had arrived at the place I'd been told everyone wanted to be, and it was nowhere. It hurt that my husband was demanding and dictatorial, but he was much like the other men in the Grand Avenue set.

I read a book by Germaine Greer, who wrote about how women are treated in our culture. For the first time I realized that maybe there wasn't anything wrong with me. I realized that I had to take my boys and get out of that town. I had to go someplace where I could have a life that didn't require me to be part of a couple.

Mildred and Pat came to one of the Keokuk parties. It was Valentine's Day and we decided to have a fancy party. I was so preoccupied with a wandering husband and failing marriage that I didn't spend as much time with them as I wanted to.

Otis and Charles visited later that year. We had a good time, although I was still distracted and failed to discuss my concerns with Otis in any depth.

Keokuk was great for the boys, if not for me. They enjoyed our safe, quiet neighborhood. The family-oriented town provided wholesome activities, and they were on the YMCA swim team. One year a Japanese method of teaching violin was all the rage. Parental participation was required, so I tried to learn along with Harry. We did not become musicians, but we did have a good time.

In 1972 I moved, with the boys, to San Francisco, got a divorce, and became immersed in hard work at the University of California San Francisco. Living in San Francisco has been like coming home after a foreign war. I learned to ski the first winter, got season tickets to the San Francisco Opera and the American Conservatory Theater, and started reading about all the great workshops that abound in California. These many years later I still enjoy those things, as well as the great California weather and the tolerant political attitudes prevalent in the Bay Area.

My career at UCSF has been interesting, challenging, rewarding, and heartbreaking, sometimes all at once. The biggest challenge is maintaining devotion to my work in the face of over twenty years of invisibility and inaudibility. Not seen, not heard, forced to abandon any pretext of involvement in university life other than clinical care. It's a good thing that patient care is my first love. I belong to all the groups considered marginal by the academic elite: women (we are still not considered appropriate for higher office, the glass ceiling is in place); black (they think only the exceptional achieve); clinician (assumed to have questionable analytical skills unless one is an internist); anesthesiologists (we are procedure people, not innovative). Once a surgeon looked up at me and requested that a resident join us. He would rather have an inexperienced white male on the case than knowledge and experience in black female form.

During the first few trying years my friend Rod (see "Letting Go" on page 50) was a boost to my faltering self-esteem. We worked together and I could count on him for a reality check. We also had fun searching out clubs featuring live rock, blues, or jazz and spent many hours together on the ski slopes. My pleasure in life was connected to my friends, and Scotty and Russ frequently joined Rod and me in our quest for good food and music (see "Celebrate Life" on page 112).

As always Otis visited, met the San Francisco crowd, and joined in our city fun. Otis and Charles especially enjoyed meeting my friend Pinkie. I met Pinkie (see "Middle-Age Spread" on page 16), a nurse, my first day at work in San Francisco. From a lukewarm beginning we have developed a wonderful friendship. About once a year I'd decide to give a party. She helped me make plans, made clever suggestions, and, most important, helped prepare the food. We'd spend hours washing, chopping, baking, and stirring, all the while solving the problems of our families and the world. Cleaning the house became a

model of many hands making light work. She would vacuum, which I hate, and I would scrub, dust, and polish. We had someone else do windows. Discussion of men was a regular feature of work talk. She dispensed wisdom received from her mother, like "Some women think any ole piece of man is better than no man at all," and "Chile, if you hear a man say you and me and nobody else, beware, he'll be a jealous fool," and, regarding divorce, "If you want to be married you may as well keep the one you've got, they're all the same under the skin." We laughed and wondered how much to believe, a little afraid that it was all true. She is a friend, confidante, and companion.

My boys lived with their father for many years, so I had a good time being the parent who took them places. My greatest joy is that my sons have become two of my best friends. In 1986 Harry joined me on a trek in Nepal. It was a fantastic adventure. Harry had a few side adventures in Kathmandu and he told me that some Nepalese were fascinated by his hair and skin color. Apparently, at that time, African Americans were infrequent visitors.

Hill and I had our adventure many years later in 1995. We visited our cousin Marianne in Kenya, where she arranged marvelous trips for us to various regions of the country. Hill spent hours bargaining and trading T-shirts for African art and jewelry.

One summer I managed to pass Otis and Charles's true-friend test. Charles bought bargain tickets for their West Coast vacation, which turned out to have a San Francisco arrival time of two in the morning. They agreed that it required a true friend to meet a flight at that dreadful hour. I thought it was the least I could do for a lifelong buddy.

It has been so wonderful for me to visit with Otis, Lydia, and Mildred twice a year these last seven years. Otis and I have gotten together regularly since leaving Talladega and have nurtured a deep and lasting friendship. My life touched Mildred's sporadically, always maintaining a connecting thread which has now grown into a grosgrain ribbon. Lydia was lost in a sea of Christmas cards, birthday cards, and an occasional note until 1989, when our reconnection felt like a homecoming. We have talked about our jobs, our problems, our families, and moved to a special closeness that happens when heart stories are shared. My satisfaction with my professional and personal life has increased dramatically since we started our circle. They are my harshest critics and most steadfast allies. I am well loved.

Otis Holloway Owens

That I would attend Talladega College was preordained. My mother, a Talladega graduate (1931), decided early that my sister Florence and I would attend "Dega" if we were interested in majors in the liberal arts. She conceded, however, that should we be interested in studying home economics, then we would attend Tuskegee Institute. Going to Talladega meant that Florence and I were once again roommates. Florence was an exceptional mentor and guide for me as a freshman and sophomore. When I experienced problems as a sorority pledge and said that I would resign from the pledge club, she said emphatically, "If you are no longer an Ivy I am no longer an AKA because blood is thicker than green ink." This incident simply indicates the importance she felt and feels for the sisterhood that my mother called "FlorenceandOtis."

The coauthors of this book, Mildred, Marilyn, Lydia, and I, entered Talladega College as freshmen in 1954. I certainly remember the first time I met Mildred. It was on the day we all checked into Foster Hall. Unlike most freshmen, Mildred and I had been assigned to a hall with upper-class students. I was rooming with Florence, who was a junior, but I am not sure exactly why Mildred was assigned to that wing of the hall.

But on that first day at Talladega I do remember Mildred's mother being extremely concerned that Mildred's bed was so near the floor-to-ceiling window. Mama Luke remarked that she was afraid that her "baby" might fall out of the window (see "A Heavy Heart" on page 62). Florence and I found this incident amusing and we have enjoyed reminding Mildred of her mom's concern. Shortly afterward, Mildred moved to another wing of the hall, but she and I became friends and we visited back and forth. Her integrity, honesty, candor, generosity, thoughtfulness, and dependability, clearly evident then and now, have made her a cherished friend.

My first memory of Lydia was at a state 4-H Club competition. To be honest, I don't remember precisely how nor when I first met Marilyn. As I recall, Lydia and Marilyn were among the young women who were both smart, attractive, and popular. On a campus where the women outnumbered the men two or more to one, there were a few freshmen women who dated steadily. Marilyn and Lydia were among them. Marilyn had one sweetheart from the beginning of our college days until graduation. During one of our many talks, Marilyn explained to me that guys seemed most attracted to girls who are coquettish and who appeared to be "airheads." She said that you have to be able to look up in the sky and say something like, "Oh, look at that cloud—it looks like a horse's head," even if it doesn't. Marilyn was certainly no airhead, but the fact that she was always very popular says something about her acting ability. Actually, I believe that the men appreciated the fact that she was genuine, respectable, and thoughtful. These are certainly some of the qualities that I admire in her as a friend.

As sophomores Marilyn, Lydia, and I were among the young women who pledged Chi chapter of Alpha Kappa Alpha. My mother and sister also pledged AKA through Chi. (Mildred pledged a year later.) I was president of the Ivy Club and became well acquainted with each of the pledges. As Ivies we knew each others' dreams and aspirations, strengths and vulnerabilities. During those days Marilyn and I spent lots of time discussing the deeper issues of life and explored various philosophies that we were learning about in our academic courses. These discussions nourished my intellectual self and heightened my appreciation for Marilyn's serious side.

When we became juniors, Lydia and I were both history majors and took most of our classes together. She was a serious student with a wonderful sense of humor. Though there were times when I tried to admonish her for partying too much, she never let my nagging interfere with our friendship. Lydia's approach to life has been one of "live and let live." Her ability to be accepting of others without judging is a quality that I value in our friendship.

As college students we frequently visited my parents' home during such short vacations as Thanksgiving or Spring Break or on a rare weekend. On occasion I would also travel to Seneca, South Carolina, or Winston-Salem, North Carolina, to visit Marilyn or Mildred. Each summer we kept in touch with our classmates and friends by writing letters and on occasion visiting with each other. Lydia's letters were always detailed and full of news about everyone. Through the years our letters have continued to be a vital link with each other. Of course there were periods when we were more engaged with graduate school and/or attending to children and when our correspondence became sporadic and infrequent. Over the past forty years we have kept in contact through visits and telephone calls. And now we also use the fax and Internet as methods of communicating.

The years at Talladega contributed significantly to my evolving intellectual, spiritual, leadership, and creative development. Through challenging classes and daily discussions (we called them "bull sessions"), both professors and students helped to stretch my mind. Perhaps the most significant aspect of this experience are the friendships I cultivated, many of which I have nurtured over a lifetime. Through the years, keeping in touch was sometimes difficult and spasmodic, if not impossible and nonexistent. Nevertheless, I always enjoy receiving mail. Mamma kept up her letter writing until she became ill. My strong proclivity for writing letters was strongly influenced (and directed) by my mother. During periods when I was a slack letter writer, she continued to write letters and send cards to my friends. To compensate for my failure to communicate, I have tried to visit or call as I have traveled through various parts of the country. When driving, Charles and I are notorious for zigzagging across the countryside, visiting fellow "Degans" and other friends in cities along the way and frequently taking detours to remote villages to connect with others.

In 1958 we graduated from Talladega College and went our separate ways. Marilyn went to Howard Medical School, Mildred taught in Columbia, Lydia taught in Bessemer, and I was dean of girls at Southern Normal

School. Two years later, during the summer of 1960, Mildred, her friend Annie Mae, and I arranged to attend summer school in Washington. I attended Howard University and they attended American University. Marilyn was a medical student at Howard and I shared her apartment. At the end of that summer, Marilyn was to be married and I was to be her maid of honor. Being in Washington made it possible for me to help out with the last-minute wedding details. Together we made the summer a real adventure. Washington was a very exciting city. During the week we focused on our classes, but our weekends were special times. Mildred and Annie Mae came to the apartment on Fridays and we bunked on the floor. We addressed wedding invitations, went shopping and to movies, concerts, parties, and museums. Washington was a favorite destination for young blacks from the South, and it seemed as if the majority of them came from North Carolina and most of them knew Mildred. One of her friends sent bouquets of flowers to her every weekend and another provided us with rides in the taxi that he drove.

At the end of the summer we had a surprise shower for Marilyn. Annie Mae returned to Winston-Salem, Mildred went to St. Louis to see James, and Marilyn and I went to Seneca, where she was getting married. Mostly I remember the sense of freedom and fun we had during that summer. Being with Marilyn, Mildred, and Annie Mae was exciting and lively, almost a revisit to college days when we were living in the dormitory, but without the rules. Our time together validated our special bond with each other. Since Marilyn and Mildred were seriously committed to marriage (Mildred was married in March 1961), the summer afforded many conversations about our future plans.

At Talladega, students were strongly encouraged to earn professional and graduate degrees after obtaining their bachelor's degrees. I would have preferred going to school close to home since my parents could not afford to send me out of the state of Alabama to attend graduate school. In 1958 universities in the state, offering programs of interest to me, were not open to blacks. However, at the time, the state Board of Education provided funds to blacks to attend graduate and professional schools out of state. In effect these funds served to thwart blacks from seeking admission to the University of Alabama and other white institutions of higher education and possible lawsuits from them once they were denied. I considered the acceptance of the out-of-state aid a sellout of my rights. Further, I believed that accepting the aid would make me a coconspirator in the perpetuation of the illegal and immoral system of racial discrimination. In good conscience I could not accept these funds. Consequently, I pursued scholarships, fellowships, and admission to private universities in the North, and was awarded a graduate assistantship at Syracuse. My dad was so proud that he kept a copy of my grades in his pocket; when anyone asked about me, he would pull it out. In 1962 I earned the Master of Arts degree in student personnel administration from Syracuse University.

The ultimate irony in my life, and one of the most satisfying, was my employment by the University of Alabama as an associate in the Institute of Higher Education Research and Services. The eleven wonderful years I spent living and working at the University and living in Tuscaloosa, Alabama, served to vindicate the indignities I suffered earlier as a citizen of Alabama.

To know me you must first know my parents, because

they have figured prominently in determining who I am today. Mamma, Edna Mae Weiss Holloway, was a beautiful, intelligent, creative, industrious, and caring person (see "Final Journey" on page 59). Born in Demopolis, Alabama, the oldest of four children, she attended Lincoln Normal School in Marion, Alabama, and graduated from Talladega College with a major in biology. Daddy, Elias Brown Holloway, Jr., was born in Greenville, South Carolina, the eighth of nine children. He came to Alabama to study agriculture at Tuskegee Institute. Mamma and Daddy met in Union Springs, Alabama, where she was a teacher and he was an agricultural extension agent. As a young man he was handsome, debonair, ambitious, and the owner of an automobile, which made him even more attractive to my mother.

My parents were secretly married in October 1933. In those days teachers in Bullock County, Alabama, were not allowed to be married. During the years when Mamma could not teach in the public schools, she earned money teaching music students at home and selling produce from Daddy's garden. She determined the size of a nickel bunch of greens by the size of the family buying it. Mamma always sold a bunch of greens big enough to feed the family, regardless of their number.

In 1947 Daddy was hired as the assistant superintendent and later appointed superintendent of the Alabama Industrial School, a facility for delinquent boys and girls in Mt. Meigs. Mamma taught and worked as a clerical assistant in Daddy's office. The campus, set in a rural environment, was our home. They retired after twenty-three years of service in 1970. Dad died in 1976 in a hospital in Montgomery, Alabama. Mamma died in 1994 in a nursing home in Birmingham.

My brother Milton Brown Holloway and I were born January 29, 1937, in the John A. Andrew Hospital on the Tuskegee Institute campus. Two days later Milton died. I once wrote a poem which expressed my feelings of being a twinless twin. As a child I felt both the closeness of his presence and emptiness of his absence in my life. (Sure wish I could remember the poem now!) I attribute my enjoyment of being close to other people to the physical closeness my twin and I shared in our mother's womb.

Two years prior to my birth my sister Florence Marie was born (see "Mamma Transformed" on page 55). As children we were inseparable, and we have always been close. Our mother used to dress us alike until Florence grew tall and slim and I remained short and grew wide. (Finally she has also grown wide.) Florence was the one to stay close to home. For a while she was a teacher and my father's secretary. During the time when her children were young she was a full-time mother. When she married Bertram Nelson Perry in 1957, I was her maid of honor, and she was my matron of honor when I married Charles in 1968. Florence's children, Donna Maria and Bertram, are special members of my family. I felt honored on Donna's wedding day when she said that she had two mothers-of-the-bride.

My early years were spent in Union Springs and Mt. Meigs, Alabama. Memories of the years in Union Springs are a mixture of delight, difficulty, and danger. I remember the pure delight of fun times under our giant pecan tree in the backyard, playing games, going for walks in the neighborhood, visiting neighbors. None of our family lived in Union Springs, but relationships were so close that some folks seemed like family. My sister's godparents, Zen and Bryant Foster, lived with my parents for a while when they first got married. My son was named for Uncle Bryant. Willie Mae Robinson (Sims) spent so much time at our house, she felt like a big sister. Mamma certainly loved her as a daughter. My closest childhood friend was Mary Paulk, who lived across the street from us. Daily we must have crossed that street a hundred times. Few people owned cars, so the street was quite safe. Clentine, the home extension agent, taught me to fish. What I enjoyed most was driving in the country or talking with Daddy as he worked in his garden. He talked about politics, religion, and the facts of life. He raised chickens and cows and sold vegetables to the grocery stores from the large garden he cultivated. Yet he always seemed to have time to talk and play with us children. These experiences paved the way for my active leadership in the 4-H Club at the local and state levels.

The most difficult period of my life was at age six when I had pneumonia and numerous complications including a collapsed lung, a heavy-duty infection, and surgery. I spent an entire month in the hospital and was a very sick child. This illness left me with very little hair and a severe curvature of the spine. In the hospital Mamma seemed to always be by my side. If I awakened during the night, she would be sleeping in a chair with her head on my bed. Our family physician, Clifton J. Gomez, was dedicated and attentive to my recovery. He made house calls and often refused payment for his services. Once he told my mother that he would take care of my medical problems until I got married. Recuperation and rehabilitation lasted for a year, so I did not attend school in the second grade. Instead, I was taught each afternoon by Ruby Thorn (Lott), my first-grade teacher.

Mamma and Daddy seized upon every chance to make ordinary daily experiences learning opportunities.

Living in Alabama in the 1940s was indeed dangerous. I was aware of the terrors of racial oppression at a very early age. The first school I attended was a decaying and deteriorating four-room building. The floors of two rooms were so rotten that they could not be used for classes. Despite warnings, children would chase each other through the rooms and sometimes fall through the deteriorated wood. Our first-grade teacher was exceptional and creative. Since the system did not provide any books for the "Negro" children, Miss Thorn wrote lessons and assignments on the blackboard and used the Sears Roebuck catalog for instruction.

One of my earliest memories is seeing blood on a path where a young black soldier had been gunned down for no good reason. He had dared to speak disrespectfully to a policeman. The day that my father saw a friend lying dead in his restaurant, killed by policemen, he decided it was time for us to leave Union Springs. In later years Daddy told me that as Florence and I began to mature, he felt that it was going to be impossible for him to protect us in a town where the policemen were so openly brutal to black folks.

Education has always been an important value in my family. My parents valued education highly and expressed concern that the public school that we attended in Mt. Meigs was not accredited. In the 1950s there were only about five high schools that black children could attend in Alabama that were accredited by the Southern Association. Southern Normal School (SNS) was one of the five. When we entered the tenth grade, Florence and I were sent to boarding schools. Florence attended Immanuel, a private Lutheran High School in Greensboro, North Carolina, and I attended SNS in Brewton, a private school supported by the Reformed Church in America. The SNS experience provided me with a strong academic and spiritual experience.

My strong work ethic was derived from watching my parents' work habits. According to Daddy, he had his first job at age five driving a wagon to pick up dirty clothes from the homes of white families and deliver them to the homes of blacks where they were washed. As a child I sold crocheted doilies and earrings made by my mother. In addition, we had specific daily chores, including cooking, churning milk to make butter, and delivering milk and butter. When I attended boarding school, all the students were required to work on campus and earn a portion of their room and board. Essentially, I have adopted the work ethic of my parents throughout my life. Since graduating from college, I have worked continuously except for approximately two years during my pregnancy and after Bryant's birth. I decided to stay home and care for Bryant until he was about eighteen months old. Watching Bryant grow and develop was a special time for me. Not only was this an important time for us to bond, but it also gave me the opportunity to direct his experiences and to instill positive values during his most impressionable years.

For two years at Syracuse I was a "student dean," an experience that set the stage for my career. Most of my work experiences have centered around student personnel administration, though the titles have evolved from counselor to assistant vice president for student affairs. The locations of my work experiences parallel those of an itinerant Methodist minister. In addition to Syracuse, I lived in Albany, Georgia; Pine Bluff, Arkansas; Charleston, West Virginia; Washington, D.C.; Albuquerque, New Mexico; Middleton, Wisconsin; Richmond, Virginia; Tuscaloosa, Alabama; and Jacksonville, Florida. But of all these, I still consider Alabama my home.

Influencing threads of my life include understanding the value of relationships with family and friends. The value of family relationships was shaped by the large extended families that got together at my grandparents' homes (in Demopolis, Alabama, and Greenville, South Carolina). As the generation of my grandparents died, family members spread out all over the continental United States no longer had a sense of a place where they could meet. I was ecstatic when my cousin Lettie Mae Ross organized the first Weiss-Sledge family reunion in Montgomery, Alabama, in 1976. Mamma's paternal family (Weiss-Sledge) holds a reunion every other year in various cities, wherever a family member is willing to take on the task of coordination. Maintaining family connections is not only enjoyable, but I see it as a responsibility.

Worshiping God and attending church were pathways to my spiritual development. As a family we attended church almost every Sunday. I remember being active in church programs as a young child and as I got older when my parents had to work on Sundays, Florence and I would take the Greyhound bus into the city to attend Sunday school and church. I have taught Sunday school, served on the vestry, and represented my congregation at diocesan conventions. All of these experiences have made me a stronger Christian.

Although my early years were heavily influenced by my parents and family, Charles E. Owens has been my inspiration since our marriage in 1968 (see "Learning to Cope" on page 45). He is my partner, my friend, my lover, my companion, my husband. I call him "Sugar Wugar" and he calls me "Honey Bunny."

Together we are the parents of a son, Bryant Holloway Owens, born January 11, 1970, in Madison, Wisconsin. In the truest sense, we produced a magnificent son. Early on, we decided on the goals of our parenting and set out to be a team in the upbringing of Bryant (see "Late-Life Parental Frustration" on page 32). Charles was one of the best Little League and tennis "moms" of all time. I was the one who always encouraged Bryant to address these activities as only a game in the scheme of life. From his birth, he has been a special joy to me. I acquired a daughter two years ago when he married Maria Marino (see "Wedding Vows" on page 102). She is a wonderful young woman who fits into our family beautifully.

Charles and I were also long distance parents to Chris Edward and Charles Douglas, sons from Charles' first marriage. They are both married and each has a son of his own. When Chris and Lynn were married in Stockton, California, my friends, Marilyn, Mildred, and Lydia, were there for the celebration of their marriage (see "Supportive Sisters" on page 165).

In 1989 three of my friends and I set out to explore ideas surrounding our plans for the future. We had all graduated from Talladega College. Maintaining contact with them has been particularly important to me. Mildred, Marilyn, and I have visited each other in our homes in various locations. I attended both of their weddings and they mine. I am godmother to Mildred's sons, and she and James are godparents to Bryant. They drove to

Madison when Bryant was baptized. One summer Mildred's family and ours (including Chris and Chuck) went to Disney World and the Bahamas for a vacation. Along the way, in Miami, Mildred and I attended the Talladega College Regional Conference while Charles and Pat baby-sat with the five boys. Lydia and I managed to stay in contact through Florence while I was living out of the state. However, once I returned to Alabama we would see each other at conferences or workshops, at Talladega College functions, or through telephone calls. Significant life events—holidays, births, deaths, graduations, acceptances into college—were occasions for each of us to dash off a letter.

In 1989 we four friends found ourselves at that stage in our lives when we were facing numerous changes and transitions and decided to hold hands and form a circle. The result is *Wearing Purple*.

Mildred Lucas Patterson

E ven though there was a wonderful teachers' college in Winston-Salem, North Carolina, my mother (at the urging of a dedicated teacher) chose Talladega for me in 1954. She wanted me to experience campus life and all of its benefits. A small college founded in 1867 (two years after the end of the Civil War), Talladega College in Talladega, Alabama, was a family-style, historically black college filled with strong friendships. It was there that I met my *Wearing Purple* friends, Otis, Marilyn, and Lydia.

I represent the first generation in my family to graduate from college. I am the youngest child in a family of six children. My mother, Lula Smith Lucas, and my father, James Arthur Lucas, believed in education. Their priorities were set around higher education for all of their children. My sister Veen died in her senior year of college and my sister Wanda chose married life after three college years. My brothers—Jake, Jack, and Clif—have embarked upon separate careers, which made them self-sustaining adults. So has my sister, Wanda, who retired from the Headstart program in 1994. Being African American in rural South Carolina, my parents witnessed many inequities that they thought were the result of limited education. They pounded into our heads that we should "go to college so that life will be better and good jobs plentiful." They wanted their children to always reap financial gain from their hard work.

In elementary school, I was the one who missed the school bus and ended up outrunning it so that I would make it to school on time to lead devotion for the day. There I had strong teachers who influenced my life. My Negro History teacher always emphasized a positive self-concept. He would say, "Miss Lucas, be the best that you can be and never let anyone turn you around." He also said, "Don't get too old to do well because age is not your friend." However, at this writing I am having the best time of my life.

Talladega College was a rare college environment. That family-style dining with black suit–clad waiters impressed me greatly. Dining-hall tables were assigned, which put us in close touch with our tablemates, and in some instances this closeness developed into long-lasting friendships. We were able to sit together with our friends after a busy day. These ties have matured into a Talladega College Grand Reunion every three years. Here we catch up on the gossip and enjoy the success stories of our schoolmates. Talladega has a reputation for sowing strong professional seeds which produce strong, towering professional people.

It was at Talladega that I chose to join Alpha Kappa Alpha sorority, where my ties became even stronger with my *Wearing Purple* friends. The closeness helped me to develop social skills. Working on campus to supplement my tuition also provided a social outlet. I remember distinctly the pleasure I got when the fraternity brothers serenaded the sorority sisters. They sent a powerful message in song. It was one of the highlights of my college days.

My *Wearing Purple* friends and I used to enjoy sharing our experiences with each other. We were strong, caring individuals who counseled each other on male-female relationships or served as a sounding board when one needed a listening ear. I have always been a great listener who believed that each life has purpose, all equally meaningful. Our personalities complemented each other, and our circle bonded for life.

As I reflect on my Talladega years, I experienced the best of times and the worst of times. I remember December 1, 1955, my sophomore year, when Rosa Parks

refused to give up her seat to a white man on a Montgomery, Alabama, bus. During the renowned boycott that followed, Martin Luther King, Jr., was invited by Alpha Phi Alpha fraternity (of which he was a member) to speak at Talladega. He talked eloquently, explaining the boycott strategies and his philosophy for change. After his speech, the message was clear and we Talladega students stood ready to reshape the Civil Rights movement.

So it is no wonder I had a cultural shock when in 1958, after completing my college degree in elementary education, I started to work for the Columbia, South Carolina, school system. I thought the successful Montgomery bus boycott had cured the world of Jim Crowism, but I soon realized that each state has its own problems and solutions. As I boarded the bus to go to work the first day, I impulsively took a vacant seat three rows from the driver. "Hey you," the bus driver said, which I ignored. In an instant he walked back and touched me on the shoulder and asked if I could read a sign saying COLORED FOLKS TO THE REAR. I continued to ignore him, since I was the only African American on the bus at that time. I continued to sit there as he used racial slurs. I remained silent and remembered the message Dr. King had given us in college. As the bus approached the end of the line, I got off before the driver could enforce his segregated laws. That was a rude awakening for me. I soon started sending teaching applications to Winston-Salem, North Carolina. There I knew I could ride the bus uninterrupted because Winston-Salem had a bus service that was *black-owned*. I was fortunate to be hired by the Forsyth County School System, and I enjoyed working at Carver Consolidated School until I married in 1961 and moved to St. Louis, Missouri.

In 1960 my *Wearing Purple* friends and I had a summer to remember in Washington, D.C. Marilyn was enrolled in Howard University Medical School, Otis was attending graduate school there, and my lifelong friend Annie Mae and I were attending graduate school at American University. We lived on campus and spent weekends fellowshipping with Marilyn and Otis in the apartment they shared: This was a clean, fun-loving environment where friends would stop by for a wholesome good time. By then I had lost all of those Talladega pounds I gained while a student. I had cut back on my calories, exercised regularly, and was now trim and noticeable to my male friends who had only been casual buddies. That was a fun-filled summer. It's no wonder that we treated the summer of 1960 as if it were our last single summer. It was for Marilyn and me. Marilyn was married in August 1961. I had met James H. Patterson, Jr., after his stint in the Air Force, in March 1961. We had a whirlwind courtship and married the following March.

In 1961 James and I relocated to St. Louis, Missouri, where he became an administrator in the Department of Oncology at Washington University Medical School and I became a teacher with the St. Louis public schools. We spent time getting to know each other and planning our family, which was important to James after the death of his parents at a very young age. In 1963, James H. Patterson III was born. Being the firstborn, he was our pride and joy. He had a great personality. We began to map out his course in life, which included the tradition of college education that had been instilled in us at an early age. Four years later, on January 19, 1967, Roger Lindsay Patterson, our second son, arrived. We immediately recognized his individuality. We continued to map out each son's educational course, which included Montessori preschool training. Each son had a different personality, but each remained focused on educational aspirations. As each progressed, James enjoyed athletics and Roger loved the academics. Both sons excelled in school. We were proud of their progress and they never gave in to peer pressure.

Otis was chosen to be our sons' godmother, a role she took seriously. She was always on call to serve as a surrogate mother when needed.

After our last son was born, my husband encouraged me to enter graduate school to earn the master's degree I so desired. I applied for a special fellowship with a stipend. I was selected along with thirty others out of a total of nine hundred applicants who spanned the continent. This program enabled me to expand my teaching skills and exchange teaching strategies with other teachers.

With thirty-four productive teaching years, I know that I am coming of age because I am now teaching the children and grandchildren of some of my former students.

Each time I think about retirement, I have a change of heart because I really enjoy my work. I am enjoying a new experience, motivational reading for reluctant readers. Implementing this concept has rejuvenated me. So at this writing, I really don't know when the "real notion" will strike me to retire. Still feeling young, I intend to enjoy a full life after my teaching career. I plan to fulfill my dream of self-employment.

Thinking about my retirement reminds me of a quote that my mother used to assist us in decision making:

Standing at the foot of the mountain,
Gazing at the sky,
How do you expect to get there
If you don't try?

I will probably go to sleep one night and decide that it is time to close the final curtain on my career.